WORD BY WORD

101 ways to inspire and engage students by
building vocabulary, improving spelling, and enriching reading,
writing, and learning

Larry Swartz

Pembroke Publishers Limited

Dedication
To my brother Stan, who solves a Jumble™ Word Puzzle each and every day

© 2019 Pembroke Publishers
538 Hood Road
Markham, Ontario, Canada L3R 3K9
www.pembrokepublishers.com

Distributed in the U.S. by Stenhouse Publishers
www.stenhouse.com

Funded by the Government of Canada
Financé par le gouvernement du Canada | Canada

Library and Archives Canada Cataloguing in Publication

Swartz, Larry, author
    Word by word : classroom strategies that enrich student learning by inspiring, engaging, and expanding their word knowledge / Larry Swartz.

Includes bibliographical references and index.
Issued in print and electronic formats.
ISBN 978-1-55138-338-5 (softcover).--ISBN 978-1-55138-938-7 (PDF)

    1. Vocabulary--Study and teaching (Elementary). 2. Vocabulary--Study and teaching (Elementary)—Activity programs. I. Title.

LB1574.5.S92 2019   372.44   C2018-905900-1
                                       C2018-905901-X

Editor: Kat Mototsune
Cover Design: John Zehethofer
Typesetting: Jay Tee Graphics Ltd.

Printed and bound in Canada
9 8 7 6 5 4 3 2 1

Contents

Foreword: Why Words Matter

This new book by Larry Swartz celebrates the power of words in helping children become literate, effective, and compelling communicators. As teachers, we want to build in our students an awareness of how words work, when and why their choices of words matter, and why a strong vocabulary deepens their impact as speakers and writers. This book offers teachers a wonderful collection of strategies and activities for achieving these outcomes with children in every stage of growth from early childhood to the middle years.

Larry knows words, and he knows how to bring word power to our students. His years as a classroom teacher, a language-arts consultant, and a teacher's college instructor, and his success as a writer of books for children and teachers—all have provided him with a true understanding and recognition of the reasons for embedding word knowledge and word awareness in our students' lives as developing readers, writers, and speakers. Words matter, and the more words students know and use, the better their abilities as effective communicators.

When listening to young people, I am always surprised by the words and phrases they have absorbed from media and social messaging. We want to promote this kind of active engagement with language, recognize the words they bring from home and community, and add to their vocabulary new and unusual words from our reading and talking together. As students interact with the rich world of print, they explore and discover all kinds of words that may become part of their language repertoire, gaining more meanings and information about the use and misuse of English. Larry Swartz' extensive collection of picture books, novels, and poems provides him with a myriad of resources to draw upon as he offers us dozens of ideas for putting word power into practice.

We want children to write as often as possible, using their word knowledge to encode their thoughts, always ready to attempt to incorporate the wide world of words into their written work, never afraid to use a difficult word for the first time, prepared to revise later. Larry presents us with many suggestions for acquiring all kinds of words to strengthen student writing, to become "worders" who will treasure the excitement of finding and choosing the exact words and phrases to breathe life into their writing.

We want children to enter the world of text, oral and printed, with wonder and surprise, reveling in the power and joys of words that matter; to play with them, embroider them, taste them on their tongues; to become language archeologists who dig for origins and changes in word forms and word-family connections. And for this to happen, we can thank Larry for all the stimuli and knowledge that his book offers.

Anne Lamott relates a story in her book *Bird by Bird*, a treatise on the world of writing:

> Thirty years ago, my older brother, who was ten years old at the time, was trying to get a report on birds written that he'd had three months to write. It was due the next day. We were out at our family cabin in Bolinas, and he was at the kitchen table close to tears, surrounded by binder paper, and pencils, and unopened books on birds, immobilized by the hugeness of the task ahead. Then my father sat down beside him, put his arm around my brother's shoulder, and said: "Bird by bird, Buddy. Just take it bird by bird."

And thus the title of this book, *Word by Word*. We grow as wordsmiths word by word, over time. As teachers, we need to be reminded constantly of ways to expand and enrich the language lives of our students. This book will nudge and motivate us into providing a stronger environment for building word power in our classrooms, so that we will see and hear students exploring new ways of making meanings with words newly-found, polished smooth by use, and remaining deep inside their word banks forever.

David Booth
Professor Emeritus, OISE–University of Toronto

Introduction

To give the children of the world the words they need, is in a real sense to give them life and growth and refreshment.
— Katherine Paterson, *Gates of Excellence*

We all know a lot of words.

We say words, write words, delight in words, puzzle over words, deliberate over word choices, greet each other with a single word, tell our own stories with words, tell stories of others with words, play with words, ask about words. Sometimes we hang on every word and sometimes we eat our words. We sing, act, chant, interpret, whisper, mince, spread, text, explain, instruct, report, and investigate words. Bill Moore informs us that we can "taste words." For Mother Teresa, "Kind words can be short and easy to speak, but their echoes are truly endless." We choose our words carefully. We put in a good word. We keep our words. We use our words.

As I worked on *Word by Word* over the last year, I became more and more fascinated with words—I listened to and read words as I hadn't ever done before. I kept a journal recording unfamiliar vocabulary I encountered in my reading and listening. I subscribed to an app that greeted me with a Word of the Day. I thought more carefully about words, old and new, familiar and strange, simple and sophisticated. I have become somewhat obsessed about noticing and collecting words. From watching the game show *Jeopardy*, I encountered such words as *suricata* and *quahogs*. From Pinterest, I learned about *pinion*, *piñata*, *pinnacle*, *pinafore*, and *pinniped*. This week, in my word journal, I noted the words *pantoum* (a type of poem), *anamnesis* (remembering of things), *lepidopterist* (butterfly and moth collector), and *recidivism* (the tendency of a criminal to reoffend)—words from the novel I was reading, a magazine article, and the news on TV. I listed the words *Worcestershire*, *mulligatawny*, and *sarsaparilla* because they seemed fun to say out loud. As part of my inquiry, I approach colleagues and ask them to share their favorite (or most interesting) word. Most friends say, "I never really thought about words until you asked me." Exactly! As a classroom teacher, a lover of children's literature, and a literacy instructor, I hope to help others think about words. And then think more about words. And develop an inquisitiveness and passion for the world of words that fills our lives, that connects us.

Without words we cannot reveal our thoughts out loud or in writing, or understand what we read. Without words we cannot succeed in having conversations with others, processing ideas, displaying what we've learned, or exploring new knowledge. Knowing and using words is at the core of our lives and at the core of student learning in school, in every subject area. When we educate students about words and nourish their word power, we encourage them to

- develop strategies for meeting new words in their reading
- see the humor in wordplay
- participate in discussions on a variety of topics (with peers and with adults)
- enhance their writing
- enrich communication skills when using social media
- investigate meanings of new words, building knowledge and understanding
- recognize and understand connections in spelling patterns
- demonstrate what they know in quizzes and/or standardized assessments

When students become more curious about language and are better able to appreciate and enjoy the beauty of it, all aspects of learning become more engaging and effective. Words matter, as they can be the key to unlocking students' desire to communicate and to opening up their involvement in their learning.

The chapters in this book provide a framework for educators (and parents) to go beyond weekly spelling tests and vocabulary busywork. They offer key strategies for making words the core of classroom instruction and engagement:

Chapter 1: Becoming a Word Collector
- Thinking about and working with words to ignite exciting learning

Chapter 2: Becoming Word Wise
- Building vocabulary and investigating meaning to increase student involvement in communication and learning

Chapter 3: Does Spelling Count?
- Spelling power to ensure effective communication

Chapter 4: The Write Word
- Writing to provide opportunities to explore the power of the word

Chapter 5: Reading the Words We Need
- Word recognition and the ability to process unfamiliar words to increase reading fluency and enjoyment across the curriculum

Chapter 6: The Poetry of Words
- Reading, writing, responding to, and chorally dramatizing poems to increase investment in word impact

Chapter 7: What Does That Mean?
- Investigating where words come from and how they develop to increase ability and excitement in using them

Chapter 8: Word Play
- Exploring wordplay and playing word games to boost student engagement with language

Chapter 9: What a Wonderful Word!
- Celebrating words to engender a love of words

- Solving word puzzles to increase understanding of spelling patterns and enrich a facility and fascination with words.

As it was for Max Brand, my goal in teaching about vocabulary is to help students become "word savvy": the word-savvy student is curious about words as they marvel about and question words they hear, read, and write. When we encourage students to become surprised or puzzled by the spelling patterns, pronunciation, and the origin of words, and to feel successful when composing written work or expressing themselves in words aloud, we are helping them to commit to learning of all kinds, as it becomes more engaging, enjoyable, and effective.

Book by book. Page by page. Word by word.

Acknowledgments

To the guest voices who shared their In the Classroom experiences with me: Cassie, Cathy, Elaine, Ernest, Heather, Rachael, Shona, Sue, Tara.

To Adrienne Gear for her literacy power and her scoops of ice cream.

To Oriana Brodziuk, OISE Teacher Candidate, whose research project gave me food for thought about vocabulary instruction.

To Sonja Dunn, who finds joy in words.

To Jo Phenix and Doreen Scott-Dunne, who helped me make sense of spelling instruction.

To Peter H. Reynolds for giving us Jerome, the Word Collector.

To David Booth, for planting and cultivating wordseed with me.

To those who allowed me to reproduce words and images in this book:

Cover of *My Skin: Brown* by @studentAsim; by permission of the author.

Cover of *Bird Guy* by David Booth, poems by David Booth; by permission of the author.

Poets as Wordsmiths from *Poems Please!* by David Booth and Bill Moore; by permission of the authors and Pembroke Publishers.

"Listen to the Rain" from *All Together Now* by Sonja Dunn; reprinted by permission of the author.

Poems by Sheree Fitch; by permission of the author.

Vocabulary and Triple-Scoop Words from *Writing Power* by Adrienne Gear; by permission of the author and Pembroke Publishers.

Lyrics from "Show Me" from *The Sound of Music* by Alan Jay Lerner; by permission of the estate of Alan Jay Lerner.

Poem from *Island Rhymes* by Jenny Nelson; by permission of the author.

"Sound of Water" from *What Is That Sound?* by Mary O'Neill. Copyright 1966. Reprinted by permission of M. Reiner.

Cover of *The Book Collector* by Peter H. Reynolds; by permission of Scholastic Inc.

"Pounding" from *Ebb & Flow* by Heather Smith; reprinted with permission of Kids Can Press, Toronto, ON.

1

Becoming a Word Collector

Selig loved everything about words—the sound of them in his ears *(tintinnabulating)*, the taste of them on his tongue *(tantalizing)*, the thought of them when they *percolated* in his brain *(stirring!)*, and most especially, the feel of them when they moved his heart *(Mama!)*.

—from *The Boy Who Loved Words* by Roni Schotter, illustrated by Giselle Potter

collect
- **to bring or gather together (things, typically when scattered or widespread)**
- **to accumulate and store over a period of time**
- **to systematically seek and acquire (items of a particular kind) as a hobby**

What in your life have you collected, do you now collect? Many of us—including young people—are collectors of things: stamps, coins, plush toys, dolls, figurines, comics, spoons, snow globes, etc. The goal of this chapter is to have students become word collectors so they can store them, use them, marvel in them, and expand their knowledge about them.

The strategies and activities in this chapter are designed to help students contemplate why words matter in their everyday lives, and how collecting words can be a significant habit/hobby that can lead to better success in reading, writing, and speaking. Here we will begin the journey of navigating the world of words, a journey that will unfold, not only as students explore strategies outlined in subsequent chapters, but also as they continue throughout their lives. The goals of this chapter include

- suggesting classroom events that inspect words day by day
- planting the seeds of becoming a word collector
- nourishing a fascination with the look, the sounds, and the meanings of words
- cultivating a love of words
- considering the alphabet as a way of learning and organizing words
- igniting students to become word gatherers as they read for pleasure, for information

10 Strategies for Collecting Words

Extension: Students can interview a parent or relative to find out what their favorite word is and why it is their favorite.

The picture book *The Very Kind Rich Lady and Her One Hundred Dogs* by Chinlun Lee tells the story of one woman who calls out the names of one hundred dogs; e.g., Fifi, Lola, Yogurt, Bingo.

1. Encourage children to become word collectors by providing them with their personal Word Collecting booklets. Students can collect words that they view (in the environment), hear (in conversations and discussions), and read (independently in books).

2. Students complete the following sentence stem:

   My favorite word is _____
   because…

   These word choices can be shared in a class discussion or be displayed in a class blog or bulletin board.

3. Invite students to suggest names of pets they know. These names can be listed on a chart. Survey the class to determine the favorite name for a pet.

4. Create a classroom bulletin board entitled We Collect Words. Using sticky notes or strips of paper, students can record new, strange, or interesting words they wish to share with others.

5. Challenge students to collect ten to twelve words on a specific topic (names of places, colors, feelings) or a spelling pattern (three-syllable words, words with two different vowels, long words). Students can put an asterisk beside the three most interesting words on their list.

6. Students write three favorite words on a piece of paper. Papers are put into a hat, box, or jar. Students gather in a circle and each selects a slip of paper. Students choose their favorite of the three words on the slip to share with classmates.

7. Invite students to focus on a specific topic or spelling pattern. Challenge students to go on a word hunt for words that fit the pattern.

8. Collect paint samples from a local hardware store. If possible, provide each student with a single sample strip. Which color name is their favorite? As a follow-up, challenge some students to invent new names for colors (for crayons or markers, ice cream flavors, or nail polish).

9. Have students collect favorite words over a one-week period and display them alphabetically on a word wall. As a follow-up activity, survey students to find out which of the collected words are their favorites. Display five favorite words and have students vote on their favorite among them. Results can be tabulated on a graph.

10. Students complete sentence stems, listing words on a specific topic:

    My favorite smell is _____.
    My favorite crayon color is _____.
    One word to describe me is _____.
    The longest word I know that begins with the letter *S* is _____.
    Here is a four-syllable word I know: _____
    Here is a word I know with three different vowels: _____

Using Picture Books about Word Collectors

Most picture books are word treasuries, in which students meet familiar words, are surprised by new words, and are impressed with the way an author has put words together to arouse emotions or create pictures in the head. When reading aloud to children, the picture book seems to be the most accessible artifact for sharing, since the format allows much (narrative, visual images, vocabulary, etc.) to be shared in an economical amount of time. Picture books also predominate the independent reading habits of most primary children. Whether reading to, reading with, or listening to a child read, using picture books with students serves as a high-priority strategy for enriching reading—and word—power.

As the hero of Peter H. Reynolds' picture book, Jerome delights in inspecting, and collecting and filling his scrapbooks words that he hears, that he sees, that he reads. No teacher guide is needed for using this book with young people. Reynolds presents an invitation to readers young and old to pay attention (and collect) words that are short, that are sweet; words that puzzle or mystify; words that are simple; words that are powerful; words that are marvelous to say; words to enrich our language power and to carry in our language backpacks to take out as needed when reading, writing, and conversing. Reynolds (and Jerome) lead readers into thinking about and reaching for their own words to make their worlds better.

A number of picture books are specifically written to celebrate engagement with words. For preschool children there are several titles available to help them identify, name, and label things. Many picture books have also been written to demonstrate how words are important in the lives of the fictitious characters, words that enrich their vocabulary and word knowledge.

"Reach for your own words to tell the world who you are and how you will make it better."
— from *The Word Collector,* Peter H. Reynolds

Bookshelf: Picture Books about Word Collectors

Learning about Words (ages 2 to 5)

Eric Carle. *My Very First Book of Words*
Jamie Lee Curtis; illus. Laura Cornell. *Big Words for Little People*
Lucy Cousins. *Maisy's Amazing Big Book of Words*
Xavier Deneux. *Touch: My Big Touch-and-feel Word Book*
Anna Dewdney & Reed Duncan. *Llama Llama Loves to Read*
Jimmy Fallon. *Your Baby's First Word will be DADA* (also *Everything is MAMA*)
Tad Hills. *How Rocket Learned to Read*
Lynn Maslen Kertell. *Bob Books: Sight Words Kindergarten Set*
Julie Morstad. *Today*
Roger Priddy. *First 100 Words*
Faith Ringgold. *Cassie's Word Quilt*
Michelle Romo. *Frankie's Magical Day*
Richard Scarry. *Richard Scarry's Best Word Book Ever*
Jessica Spanyol. *Carlo Likes Reading*

The Power of Words (ages 6+)

Pilar López Ávila; illus. Mar Azabel. *Ayobami and the Names of the Animals*
Kate Banks; illus. Peter Sís. *Alphabet Soup*
Kate Banks; illus. Boris Kulikov. *Max's Words*
Monalisa DeGross. *Donovan's Word Jar*
Melanie Florence; illus. Gabrielle Grimard. *Stolen Words*
Debra Frasier. *Miss Alaineus: A vocabulary disaster*
Yee-Lum Mak; illus. Kelsey Garrety-Riley. *Other-Wordly: words both strange and lovely from around the world*
Jane O'Connor; illus. Robin Preiss Glasser. Fancy Nancy series
Doreen Rappaport. *Martin's Big Words*

Peter H. Reynolds. *The Word Collector*
Lora Rozler. *Words*
Roni Schotter; illus. Giselle Potter. *The Boy Who Loved Words*
Beck & Matt Stanton. *Did you Take the B from my _ ook?*
Laya Steinberg; illus. Debbie Harter. *Thesaurus Rex*
Sonja Wimmer. *The Word Collector*

Inspecting Words

"Analyzing a word—considering how its meaning connects to other words and thinking about how the word works—is brain food. Our brains literally grow when we make new connections. Tying the meaning of a word to how it is used, to situations where it is used, and to related words creates real, physical connections to the brain." (Beck and McKeown, 2018)

These whole-class activities are provided as suggestions for how students can collect and inspect words day by day. If you implement one or more of these strategies, you can help students become word collectors, increasing their vocabulary and word power. The daily routine need take only a moment or two in your language arts program. Attention can be drawn to definitions, spelling patterns, usage, and/or etymology.

1. Word of the Day App

Word of the Day online programs or apps are designed to build vocabulary and information about words. For example, the whole class or individual students can subscribe to the Merriam-Webster Word of the Day program. Each day a word is sent to the inbox and *Did you know?* facts about the English language are featured. These new vocabulary words can be featured in the class for discussion.

2. Word-a-Day Calendars

Commercial word-a-day calendars can be purchased and put on display in the classroom. Focus students' attention on a vocabulary word featured in a calendar.

3. Word Wizard

One of the classroom duties can be to assign a student to be word wizard of the day. The word wizard collects, records, and posts new or unusual words that they notice in the environment or in their reading. These words can be displayed on a whiteboard, a bulletin board, or an interactive whiteboard.

4. Solving a Word Puzzle

For word puzzles, see Chapter 10.

A featured word puzzle can be displayed in the classroom for students to solve independently or with a partner. Words chosen for the spelling puzzle could include new vocabulary words or focus on a spelling pattern.

5. Read-All-About-It Headlines

Draw students' attention to the headlines that appear on the front page of a newspaper. Students can point out unfamiliar words featured. As an alternative, students can note spelling patterns that appear in the headlines.

In the Classroom: Becoming Word Searchers
with thanks to Sue Freypons, Grade 6 Teacher

When I visited a Grade 6 classroom, I asked the students to work in groups to brainstorm questions that they had about words. Here are some examples that prompted students to become inquirers—word searchers!

- What are some *q* words that aren't followed by the letter *u*?
- How many new words are added to the dictionary each year?
- Why don't we just eliminate silent letters if they are silent anyway?
- Why does the word *Wednesday* have a *d* after the *e* when we pronounce it "Wensday"?
- Are there many words with just vowels? What is the longest word with vowels only?
- What words have the *ph* sound in the middle of the word?
- Why is a building called a building when they are already built?
- Why do some words end in *–able* and some in *–ible*?
- Are french fries French?

The next phase of the lesson focused on students finding answers to some questions about words. Each student was given a question to investigate using the Internet. Through inquiry, students searched words, their origins, and/or their definitions:

Q: What is the plural of the word *ice cream*?

A: The word *ice creams* can be used to name various types of ice cream or a collection of ice creams; e.g., *The candy story had a variety of chocolate ice creams on display*.

Q: What are some words that have all five vowels?

A: *education, automobile, evacuation*

Q: Where does the name *Canada* come from?

A: Canada comes from the Huron-Iroquois word *kanata*, meaning village or settlement.

Q: What is the difference between a homonym and homograph?

A: Homonyms are words that sound alike but have different spellings and different meanings (*knight/night*; *suite/sweet*). Homographs are words that are spelled the same but have different meanings (bear, rose).

Q: Are there any words that begin with silent letters?

A: *knowledge, knot, pterodactyl, wrist*

Investigating Silent Letters

From time to time, I present a word-collecting challenge to the students. Focusing on a specific vocabulary or spelling rule, students are encouraged to collect words they encounter from their reading, from the environment, and by searching the Internet. In this instance, I introduced a word-collecting event to help answer several students' questions about silent letters. The picture book *P is for Pterodactyl* proved to be an ideal source to present the concept of silent letters to the students.

A challenge was presented to the students: Which of the following letters is the most common silent letter: *B, H, K, T, W*? To begin, we brainstormed words with silent letters that we were familiar with. Students worked in groups of three to complete a chart, listing words with silent letters. Throughout the week, students collected and added to the chart, listing words they encountered in their reading and as they searched words on the Internet.

P is for Pterodactyl: The worst alphabet book ever: All the letters that misbehave and make words nearly impossible to pronounce by Raj Haldar & Chris Carpenter, illustrated by Maria Tina Beddia, **is a whimsical alphabet book that presents an array of words that begin with letters that are not pronounced (***H is for Heir; J is for Jai Alai,* **M is for** *Mnemonic***). A sentence accompanies each page of text to help readers say these words properly; e.g.,** *The noble knight's knife nicked the knave's knee.*

A Is for Alphabet

Research makes it clear that readers and writers require alphabet knowledge. Helping young children explore and understand the sounds and symbols of alphabetical letters is essential to literacy development. Alphabet centres for young children should include a variety of writing instruments, magnetic letters, alphabet cards or tiles, alphabet books, and sight-word lists. At the centre, students can experiment with writing by drawing and tracing letters, making rhyming words, playing alphabet games, constructing words, and creating personal dictionaries by listing words alphabetically.

For students of all ages, the alphabet is a meaningful way to classify words:

- Students can explore vocabulary on a specific topic by listing them in alphabetical order.
- Word puzzles and word games challenge students to explore words alphabetically.
- When using use a print or online dictionary, it is important that students understand how words are presented in alphabetical order to provide easy access to the definitions of words.
- Students come to understand how the alphabet is used to organize words and titles: e.g., class lists, library shelving by author, bibliography references, etc.

Primary Activities (Ages 4–7)

An Illustrated Alphabet

As a whole-class activity, students can create an illustrated alphabet. The alphabet can be made up of mixed images or it can be themed (e.g., story characters, animals, foods). For young children, ensure that the words they choose to illustrate do not begin with consonant blends; brainstorm words that begin with the letter but have a pure sound (e.g., *car* instead of *chair*). Display the completed work for easy reference.

Teaching Tips

- Older students (or buddies) can create an illustrated alphabet for younger children.
- Completed pages can be assembled into a class book for students to read independently.
- The activity can be repeated at different times of the year, exploring different spelling concepts (e.g., adjectives, two-syllable words, etc.).

Letter Sorting

Select a handful of plastic or magnetic letters for students to examine. Invite them to find letters with different features; e.g., straight lines, curved lines, tails, etc.

Survey and Graph of Alphabet Letters

Have each student write the first letter of his or her first name on a sticky note. Notes can be displayed on the wall or the board to form an alphabet graph. Which letter is the most popular? Which letters are missing from the graph?

Animal Alliteration

Provide students with a stuffed animal that can serve as the class mascot. Have students suggest alliterative names for the toy; e.g., Bodhi Bear, Big Bunny, Cool Carl, Silly Sally. Invite them to name things that this animal might like that begin with the same letter:

> Bodhi Bear likes burgers.
> He visited Buffalo.
> He likes big balloons.
> His favorite colors are blue, black, and brown.

What Word Am I?

Play this game with students by giving clues:

> I am a T word that is a red vegetable.
> I am an J word that is a kind of drink.
> I am an R word that is a large animal with a horn.

Extension: For older students, the game can be played in pairs or in teams. Students can devise challenging vocabulary questions to be asked. Score can be kept.

Junior/ Intermediate Activities (Ages 7+)

I Packed My Backpack

Each player adds one item to be "packed" in an imaginary backpack. The game is cumulative; as the brainstorming continues, each player must list in order the items that have been previously mentioned. A further challenge is to list only words that start with a single alphabet letter, words in alphabetical order, or words on a particular theme. The following example shows how the game might be played by suggesting things we read:

> Player #1: *I packed my backpack with an atlas.*
> Player #2: *I packed my backpack with an atlas and a biography.*
> Player #3: *I packed my backpack with an atlas, a biography, and a comic book.*

Alphabetical Order

Display five or six words that might appear on a single page in a dictionary. Challenge students to create a list of the words in alphabetical order.

Collaborative Alphabet Books

The alphabet provides a convenient pattern for collaborative efforts. Each student can be assigned to create a page of an alphabet book. This can be as simple as identifying nouns or verbs for each letter of the alphabet. The names of animals, authors, book titles, or countries are examples of potential alphabet book creations, as are curriculum topics (math vocabulary, science vocabulary, capital cities, ancient civilizations). Many alphabet books offer syntactic patterns that provide a suitable launch into writing: *Animalia* by Graeme Base; *Tomorrow's Alphabet* by George Shannon and Donald Crews; *A My Name is Alice* by Jane E. Bayer, illustrated by Steven Kellogg; *Miss Bindergarten Gets Ready for Kindergarten* by Joseph Slate, illustrated by Ashley Wolff.

Alphabetical Grid

Have students write the letters of the alphabet in a vertical list, or provide an alphabet grid. Students brainstorm words on a particular topic that they choose or that is assigned to them.

- names of fruits and vegetables
- names of animals
- orchestra instruments
- the body/healthy living
- cities
- things you might pack in a suitcase
- authors
- homonym pairs
- two-syllable names
- dance terms

Teaching Tips

- This activity can be done alone or in pairs.
- Students can be challenged to add more than one word for each alphabet letter.
- Students can be challenged to complete the list in a specific time limit (e.g., 5 minutes).
- Points can be scored for each word listed.
- Once lists are completed, students can use the Internet to add missing items.

Dollar Words

In the novel, *Because of Mr. Terupt* by Rob Buyea, a first-year teacher challenges his fifth-grade students to discover words that would be worth a dollar when adding up their letter values; "Not ninety-nine cents or a dollar and one cent, but one dollar exactly." Throughout the school year, Mr. Terupt's students are excited whenever they are able to solve the word problem. Examples of dollar words are *Wednesday*, *excellent*, and *grumpy*. This activity invites students to solve arithmetic problems about words. For this activity, each letter of the alphabet is worth money. Using the alphabet code, students are challenged to manipulate words, paying attention to the correct spelling of words and to words that follow a particular rule.

A = 1¢	H = 8¢	O = 15¢	V = 22¢
B = 2¢	I = 9¢	P = 16¢	W = 23¢
C = 3¢	J = 10¢	Q = 17¢	X = 24¢
D = 4¢	K = 11¢	R = 18¢	Y = 25¢
E = 5¢	L = 12¢	S = 19¢	Z = 26¢
F = 6¢	M = 13¢	T = 20¢	
G = 7¢	N = 14¢	U = 21¢	

1. How much is your first name worth?
2. How much is your last name worth?
3. How much is the word *VOCABULARY* worth?
4. *WORD + READ =*
5. *WRITING - READING =*
6. Which word is more expensive, *POETRY* or *NOVEL*?
7. Which of these words is worth a dollar: *explore, explain, explodes*?
8. How much is the capital city of Canada worth?
9. Write a word or words that would be worth 50 cents.
10. Find a dollar word that contains three different vowels.

Bonus: Using the dollar-word code, write a math problem for a friend to solve.

Bookshelf: An ABC of Alphabet Books

Check out the letters in bold, in author names or titles, to see 26 ABC books—one for each letter of the alphabet!

Susan **A**llen & Jane Lindaman; illus. Vicky Enright. *Read Anything Lately?*

Nick **B**ruel. *Bad Kitty*

Eric **C**arle. *Eric Carle's ABC*

Chris L. **D**emarest. *Firefighters A to Z*

Lois **E**hlert. *Eating the Alphabet*

Ian **F**alconer. *Olivia's ABC*

Kate **G**reenaway. *A Apple Pie*

Kellen **H**atanaka. *Work: An occupational ABC*

Mick **I**nkpen. *Kipper's A to Z: An alphabet adventure*

Oliver **J**effers. *Once Upon an Alphabet: Short stories for all the letters*

Lynn Maslen **K**ertell ; illus. Sue Hendra & John R. Maslen. *My First Bob Books: Alphabet*

Edward **L**ear; illus. Suse Macdonald. *A Was Once an Apple Pie*

Bill **M**artin, Jr. & John Archambault; illus. Lois Ehlert. *Chicka Chicka Boom Boom*

Innosanto **N**agara. *A Is for Activist*

Jane **O**'Connor & Robin Preiss Glasser. *Fancy Nancy's Favorite Fancy Words: From Accessories to Zany*

Patricia **P**olacco. *G Is for Goat*

Mary Elting and & Michael Folsom; illus. Jack Kent. ***Q** Is for Duck*

Bill **R**ichardson; illus. Roxanna Bikadoroff. *The Alphabet Thief*

Laura Vaccaro **S**eeger. *The Hidden Alphabet*

Mike **T**wohy. *Oops Pounce Quick Run: An alphabet caper*

Michael **U**lmer; illus. Melanie Rose-Popp. *M is for Maple*

Matthew **V**an Fleet. *Alphabet*

Eric **W**alters; illus. Sue Todd. *An African Alphabet*

Xavier Deneux. *TouchThinkLearn: ABC*

Teresa Anne Power; illus. Kathleen Rietz. *The ABCs of **Y**oga for Kids*

Sean Lamb; illus. Mike Perry. ***Z** Goes First: An alphabet story Z-to-A*

Word Facts by the Numbers

The facts presented help provide information about our use and understanding of words. Statistics, of course, vary, but in 2013 *The Economist* outlined some interesting facts about the average person's vocabulary (*The Economist,* Test Your Vocabulary). Many factors, including educational background, likely influence the authenticity of these numbers, but it is worth noting that these numbers are drawn from average test-takers.

- **860.3 million** The number of words the average person uses in a lifetime
- **80 000** Vocabulary of average college-educated English speakers
- **20 000–35 000** Range of vocabulary for most adult test-takers
- **20 000** Active vocabulary of an average adult English speaker
- **40 000** passive vocabulary of an average adult English speaker
- **10 000** Average vocabulary of eight-year-old test-takers
- **5000** Average vocabulary of four-year-old test-takers
- **4500** The most common vocabulary size for foreign test-takers
- **75–225** The number of words recognized by test-takers that were toddler through two years old
- **1** The number of words most adults learn every day

Exploring Word Idioms

Considering idioms using the word *word* can help students consider how a single word can be used in the English language.

1. Students can work in groups of two or three. With a time limit of three minutes, how many expressions can they brainstorm that feature the word *word* (e.g., *wordplay, mark my words*)?

2. Provide students with a copy of the Word Idioms list on page 22. Working in groups of two or three, students read the list and discuss the meaning behind each of these expressions. Which of these expressions are familiar to them? Which of them are unfamiliar?

3. Invite students to choose any five idioms and write them in a sentence that helps to explain their meaning.

> My friend talks so fast when she gets excited, with her words so close together, that it's hard to get a word in edgewise.

---

40 Ways to Collect Words: A Guide for Families

1. Notice words on T-shirts you pass by.
2. Read menu items.
3. Use magnetic letters on the fridge to build words.
4. Celebrate a Word of the Day.
5. Download a Word of the Day app.
6. Make lists together.
7. Play board games; e.g., Balderdash, Scrabble, Bananagrams, Boggle.
8. Watch *Wheel of Fortune*.
9. Notice signs on storefronts.
10. Read street signs: Which words are familiar? Which words are invented?
11. Tell a story about your name.
12. Translate words from another language.
13. Share a personal word-collecting book.
14. Have children share their word-collecting books.
15. Use the Internet to find interesting facts about words.
16. Notice word patterns.
17. Highlight words from literature that are new and/or interesting.
18. Provide a three-word dictation challenge (focus on spelling).
19. Arrange items in alphabetical order; e.g., food packages, personal libraries.
20. Play I Spy using words in the environment.
21. Buy word puzzle books; e.g., crosswords, word searches.
22. Create word puzzles collaboratively.
23. Inspect newspaper headlines.
24. Read labels on packages.
25. Send word challenges by email, in lunch boxes.
26. Prepare and present a word scavenger hunt.
27. Read riddles together and explain punny answers as needed.
28. Play a rhyme game: How many words can you rhyme with _____ ?
29. Use a dictionary to explore words.
30. Read and follow recipes.
31. Build words using letters on car licence plates.
32. Read poems aloud.

---

33. Notice words in book titles.
34. Say tongue-twisters out loud.
35. Provide digital word games and puzzles.
36. Facilitate a word wall collecting favorite words, beautiful words, odd words.
37. Share *Did you know?* facts about words.
38. Provide information about word origins.
39. Brainstorm words on a topic; e.g., farm animals, two-syllable vegetables.
40. Ask questions; e.g., What do you think this word means? What does this word remind you of?

Word Idioms

- word up
- buzzword
- He doesn't have a kind word for anybody.
- a war of words
- a play on words
- I'm at a loss for words.
- a man of his word
- a person of few words
- have the last word
- I don't believe a word of it.
- It's beyond words.
- to go back on one's word
- Don't breathe a word.
- word of mouth
- to eat one's words
- famous last words
- fighting words
- for want of a better word
- from the word go
- can't get a word in edgewise
- to get the last word in
- Say the word.
- to hang on every word
- Sticks and stones will break my bones but words will never hurt me.
- to put a word in your ear
- to have a word with
- to have no words for
- The words stick in my throat.
- in other words
- in so many words
- Actions speak louder than words.

- to keep one's word
- to leave word for
- Many a true word is spoken in jest.
- Mark my words.
- Don't mince words.
- Mum's the word.
- Don't breathe a word.
- My word is my bond.
- or words to that effect
- A picture is worth a thousand words.
- to put in a good word
- It's hard to put into words.
- Don't put words in my mouth.
- to receive word
- Let me say a few words.
- to send word to
- to spread the word
- to swallow one's words
- Take my word for it.
- take the words right out of my mouth
- too funny for words
- Don't twist my words
- My word!
- What's the good word?
- I won't hear a word against her.
- His word is law.
- to give your word of honor
- words to live by
- It's your word against his.
- use your words
- word salad
- a word to the wise

Pembroke Publishers ©2019 *Word by Word* by Larry Swartz ISBN 978-1-55138-338-5

2

Becoming Word Wise

Monday is vocabulary day, when Mr. Daniels goes over the new words for the week. As far as reading lessons go, that isn't so bad. All I have to do is listen as he tells us the word's meaning, and I can usually remember it because I make mind movies about each one and that helps me remember.

But today, during vocabulary Mr. Daniels brings up two words: alone and lonely. He asks for volunteers to explain the difference between the two.

— from *Fish in a Tree* by Lynda Mullaly Hunt

Your *epidermis* is showing! Your *proboscis* is showing!

Often when we hear or read new words, we might not be able to make sense of what is being said because we don't understand what the words mean. We can often get by without knowing the word, but we most likely don't want to seem foolish or uninformed by not "getting it." If we don't know that an *epidermis* is the skin, or the *proboscis* is a nose, this joke might seem rude.

In order to be proficient users of words, we all need to have frequent encounters with new words. In the classroom, explicit instruction can provide students with a focus on vocabulary learning, but we need to go beyond a focus on word study and provide them with opportunities to be engaged with—and maintain—their vocabulary learning in a number of ways. To help students inspect and respect words, it is important that they stretch their understanding of words by meeting words they have learned beyond those that have been introduced into the word-study component of any program. To engage and enrich students' vocabulary, we also need to value that students take their learning outside the classroom, and seek examples of words they have learned elsewhere in their lives; when listening to conversations; when watching television, movies, and theatre; and when exploring the Internet.

It is significant that helping students learn new words shows them how to learn new concepts. Vocabulary instruction is both a reading skill and a writing skill,

"Texts of all kinds (print, visual, and digital) are filled with what could be fascinating ideas and information, but even if our kids are able to decode and pronounce words, they may not understand their meaning without explicit vocabulary instruction." (Overturf, Montgomery & Smith, 2013)

and may be considered particularly challenging since students are giving and receiving vocabulary while being exposed to new words and using new words themselves. In this chapter are activities that help students

- consider specialized vocabulary by preparing a glossary of terms
- increase their fascination with words by investigating some interesting word facts
- complete a quiz to consider familiarity with vocabulary and learn new vocabulary
- explore print and online dictionaries to access meanings of familiar and unfamiliar words
- consider the components of a definition by examining the dictionary and composing definitions.
- expand word knowledge by paying attention to words at school, at home, in the community

---

Four Phases of Learning Vocabulary

Jordan Catapano (TeachHub) points out that there are four unique phases of incorporating vocabulary understanding into any classroom's curriculum. Catapano uses the term "phases" to represent the slow transition from seeing a word for the first time to fully understanding a word and being able to use it.

Phase One: Monitoring Level of Familiarity

- How familiar is the student with any given word they encounter?
- Are words extremely familiar, slightly familiar, or completely new?

Phase Two: Attacking New Words While Reading

- How does the student make sense of the word (e.g., examining the root word, using a dictionary, considering the context)?

Phase Three: Learning the Definition of a New Word

- Does the student naturally understand the meaning of the word?
- Is the student able to understand the word when it is encountered in a new setting?

Phase Four: Owning the Meaning of a Word

- Does the student successfully use the word in their oral and/or written communications?

Specialized Vocabularies

Compiling and Working with Specialized Vocabularies

This list provides some suggested topics (some students might wish to choose their own topic).

Baking terms	Star Wars words
Fishing words	Terminology for a sport (e.g., soccer, hockey)
Exotic fruit names	
Theatre words	Bullying vocabulary

Celebrations around the world	Sea creatures
Instruments around the world	Geology (rocks and minerals)
In-the-hospital terms	Gaming words
Sewing terms	Tech time
Ice-skating words	Words from Harry Potter (people, places, things)
Parts of a car	
Body parts	Music words
Carpenter tools	Architecture words
Features of graphic texts	Math words

- Students choose a topic of particular interest. Using the Internet, they investigate a list of at least ten terms (and their definitions). This activity can be done by students working independently or in pairs. If working alone, students can collect at least 10 words on a topic. If working with a partner, the list of words could be longer. If each student in a class of 25 collects ten words, the class will collaboratively be collectors of 250 words that they likely didn't previously know.
- Students can work independently to list vocabulary words that are particular to a topic of expertise or interest. They then meet with a partner to compare lists and work together to add additional words to their personal lists. Students can use the Internet to research other words that might be added to their lists.
- Students can work in groups of three or four to brainstorm vocabulary words and prepare lists on a chart within a given time period (e.g., 5 minutes). On a signal, groups rotate to a new chart and add vocabulary words. Which is the longest list in the room?

Working with Vocabulary Lists on Special Topics

- Challenge students to create an alphabetical list of terms on a topic of their choice. Can they find at least one word for each letter of the alphabet?
- Students work with a group who has prepared a different vocabulary list. Working collaboratively, students find a way to organize all the words on the lists by pattern (e.g., by syllables; words with double consonants or words with double vowels; words with one vowel, two vowels, three different vowels; etc.)
- Students create a word search puzzle for others to solve using words they've collected on a topic of interest.
- Students create a glossary of terms of ten to twelve vocabulary words by providing brief definitions of those words.
- Students post the words on a class website.
- The class can prepare a quiz (fill in the blank, true or false, multiple choice) of specialized vocabulary words, with each student contributing at least one question. Once students have submitted questions, prepare a quiz to test students' knowledge of specialized terms.
- A small group of students can gather the word lists and arrange the vocabulary in alphabetical order. In this way, a class dictionary of specialized vocabulary can be posted and shared with others.

In the Classroom: Preparing and Presenting a Glossary of Specialized Vocabulary

Tara Swartz-O'Neill, Grade 4 Teacher

Since the start of the school year, I have been working with my Grade 4 class on weekly spelling lists. Each word list focused on a particular letter blend, sound, or concept learned in class. I felt that it was good to have a spelling pattern to explore, but I wondered if these words had a meaningful context for the students to apply their understanding.

The Word Collector by Peter H. Reynolds was given to me by my teacher-librarian and proved to be an ideal spark to my word-study program. The picture book tells the story of a young boy who loves to collect words. As a class, we discussed how we are all word collectors already. Each student has spent their whole life collecting words: big words and small words, nouns and verbs, happy words and sad words, simple words and complex words.

Following the reading of the book, I explained to students that they would be creating their own spelling lists of ten or more words of their choice. As a class, we discussed what a glossary is and how it is typically used. Another picture book, *Peaceful Fights for Equal Rights*, served as a model for glossary. We came up with words that would belong in specific categories, such as baking, sports, or playing an instrument. Two students have families from Croatia, and they decided they could write out a list of Croatian words their peers have never heard before. Since we had just completed our Habitats and Communities unit in science, some students decided to define specific animals from their chosen biomes. One of my students, a competitive gymnast, chose to write a glossary of gymnastics terms. Another student is a horseback rider, and she chose to write a glossary of horseback riding terms. The students then used laptops to research and type out their words.

This was by far the most exciting vocabulary activity we did this term. First, when students learned they were going to be choosing their own spelling words, their excitement was highly evident. Once they found out that the words could be about any topic they were interested in, their minds really began racing. Every single student was keen to list words they already knew and to use the Internet to research words connected to their subject. Students were encouraged to not just copy information, but to also explain the meanings of the vocabulary terms in their own words. They were excited to be able to share their final lists with their teachers and peers. We had become word collectors and, as a community, we had more 200 new vocabulary words to exchange with each other. The students were prouder of their end products than they had ever been with a memorized spelling list. The glossary activity helped me to understand that when students are empowered and given choices they become masters of their own learning. Preparing and presenting a glossary encouraged my students to use their knowledge and expertise to teach others about new topics and to become wordhunters on an expert topic. The words became a gateway into the students' lives, hobbies, and interests, and fostered a love for vocabulary—and spelling.

Peaceful Fights for Equal Rights by Rob Sanders, illustrated by Jared Andrew Schorr, presents an alphabetic list of terms intended to help students think about taking action for peace. A glossary of terms at the back of the book provides explanations for vocabulary items spread throughout the picture book; e.g., campaign, endure, mediate, picket, vigil.

Sample Glossary

Alex's Gymnastics Glossary	
Word	**Definition**
aerial	Like a cartwheel but with no hands
Barani	A trampoline and tumbling stunt in which the performer does a front straight or tuck somersault with a half twist
cartwheel	A circular sideways handspring with the arms and legs extended
flip	To turn over with sudden quick movement
floor	The lower surface of a room, on which one may walk, that has springs under it
grips	Fabric that goes over your first three fingers and down over your palm and buckles around the wristband on your wrist. Under the piece on your palm is a dowel to help you hold onto the bar.
gymnastics	Exercises developing or displaying physical agility or coordination
handspring	A jump through the air onto one's hands followed by another onto one's feet
rebound	After one bounce it is a rebound
rings	A circular band, typically a precious metal or wood
round-off	Like a cartwheel but you keep your legs together
trampoline	A rectangular bed made of mesh that you jump on
vault	A beat board with springs in between where you run and jump on it, and land on a soft mat

Exploring Fun Word Facts

When you present students with word facts, you can arouse their curiosity about words and entice them to consider the strangeness and wonder of words. Students are encouraged to share word facts that they come across as they collect and inspect vocabulary.

- The word *asthma* begins and ends with a vowel and has no other vowels in between.
- The longest word in dictionaries having only one vowel is *strengths*.

- *Doorhinge* is the only word that rhymes with orange.
- *Chilver* (a rare word that means female lamb) is one of the few possible words that rhymes with silver.
- In the word *unimaginatively*, the vowels and consonants alternate
- *United Arab Emirates* is the longest name of a country consisting of alternating vowels and consonants.
- *Ouenouaou* is the name of a stream in the Philippines. It has nine letters and only one consonant.
- *Sequoia* is a word that contains all five vowels.
- The word *facetiously* contains all five vowels in consecutive order.
- *Aerious* is the shortest word with the five vowels occurring in alphabetical order.
- The longest common word without any of the five vowels is *rhythms*. *Tsktsk* is the longest word that doesn't contain any vowel at all (you indicate your disapproval of someone by making a tsktsk sound)
- The word *swims* is *swims* even when turned upside down.
- The name of the infinity sign is *lemniscate*. The word is Latin for "decorated with ribbons."
- *I am* is the shortest complete sentence in the English language.
- The part of a wall between two windows is called the *interfenestration*.
- A *pangram* sentence is one that contains every letter in the language.
- *Google* is a misspelling of a real-life mathematical term *googol* (a 1 followed by 100 zeros). The original name of the search engine invented by Larry Page and Sergey Brin was BackRub.
- *I, we, two,* and *three* are some of the oldest words in the English language, first appearing in medieval manuscripts. The shortest, oldest. and most commonly used word is *I*.

- Provide students with a photocopy of these facts. In groups, students can discuss which fact(s) they found to be the most interesting.
- A single word fact can be posted daily for the students to consider.

Words you can make if you have only vowels in your seven Scrabble tiles:
- *AA*: a type of lava
- *AE*: grapheme formed by the letters a and e
- *AI*: a sloth with three long claws; a branch of computer science
- *AIEEE*: a secondary examination in India
- *EUOUAE*: a medieval musical term
- *UOIAUAI*: old English word meaning "twin"

Extension: Encourage students to collect and share fascinating word facts that they encounter in the environment, in the media, and in their reading.

sesquipedalian
(adj.) having many syllables; words that are characterized by being long

"Two of the hardest words in the language to rhyme are *life* and *love*. Of all words."
— Stephen Sondheim, composer and lyricist

Long Words

Pneumonoultramicroscopicsilicovolcanoconiosis: a lung disease contracted from the inhalation of very fine silica particles, especially from a volcano (45 letters)
Antidisestablishmentarianism: opposition to the establishment of the Church of England (28 letters)

Some facts about the word *supercalifragilisticexpialidocious* (34 letters)
- It is the title a song written for the movie musical Mary Poppins.
- It is an adjective meaning extraordinarily good; wonderful.
- The word appears in some dictionaries (like Oxford) but not all.
- The song lyrics identify it as "something to say when you have nothing to say."
- The first record of the word supercaliflawjalisticexpialidoshus is its appearance in a 1931 newspaper column as a made-up word that describes "all words in the category of something wonderful." It was perhaps first used in the 1940s.
- What does it actually mean? super = above; cali = beauty; fragilistic = delicate; expiali = to atone; docious - educable: atoning for being educable through extreme beauty and delicacy

See page 32 for Vocabulary Skills Test. The correct answers to the test:
1. c); 2. b); 3. b); 4. a); 5. c); 6. a); 7. b); 8. b); 9. c); 10. a); 11. a); 12. c); 13. a); 14. c); 15. b).

"Vocabulary research strongly points to the need for frequent encounters with new words if they are to become a permanent part of an individual's vocabulary repertoire. Those encounters should not be limited to the week in which words are the focus of instruction. Rather students should have opportunities to maintain their vocabulary learning and elaborate their understanding of words by meeting words they have learned in contexts beyond the instructional ones." (Beck, McKeown, and Kucan, 2013, p. 109)

definition
late Middle English: from Latin verb *definire* "to set bounds to"
- a statement of the exact meaning of a word, especially in a dictionary
- an exact statement or description of the nature, scope, or meaning of the action

Testing Vocabulary Skills

Students can work alone or with a partner to complete the Vocabulary Skills Test on page 32. It is unlikely that students will be familiar with many of the vocabulary words, but the goal of the quiz is to

- enrich vocabulary by introducing students to new words and their meanings
- invite students to discover the definitions of one or more of these words by using the Internet or dictionary
- become curious about unfamiliar words they meet in their reading, their environment, the media

Preparing a Vocabulary Quiz

Invite students to work alone or in pairs to develop a vocabulary quiz using the multiple choice model of the Vocabulary Skills Test on page 32. Students each prepare 8 to 10 questions, highlighting vocabulary words that may not be familiar to others. Students may choose to use words connected to a particular theme or topic, as suggested on page 25. Once they have completed their own quiz, students can exchange and solve a partner's quiz.

D Is for Dictionary
Exploring a Print Dictionary

Most definitions that students need to look up can be found on the Internet. However, dictionaries and other reference materials (thesauruses, picture dictionaries, language dictionaries) should be available to students to access when they need to discover the spelling, meaning, or usage of the words they encounter in their reading and writing. Students can use dictionaries more effectively if they are familiar with the features and are presented with strategies to develop skills that are relevant to their reading and writing.

Why Use the Dictionary?
The best way to encourage dictionary use in the classroom is to provide students with a purpose for using the dictionary. Brainstorm a list of reasons for using the dictionary for supporting reading and reading. Some reasons might include

- to discover the meaning of the word
- to discover the pronunciation of the word
- to discover the history or origin of a word
- to find a synonym
- to check the spelling of a word
- to check other forms of a word, such as the past tense of a verb or the plural of a noun

Digging Into the Dictionary
Present the definition of the word *definition* (or any other word) to students and point out the features that give information about the word. Present students with an invented word, like *frod*. Invite students create a definition for this word by including

- its pronunciation

Extension: What might the definitions be for one of these words: *flazar, foxitin, frinkle, froodle, froosh*?

- the part of speech it is
- one or two definitions to explain the meaning of the word
- a sentence that includes the word for each definition
- synonyms
- an illustration (optional)

In Your Own Words

The following words have been added to online and/or print dictionaries in recent years:

avatar	multi-tasking
blog	module
gigahertz	Twitter
meme	binge-watch

Have students write a brief explanation in their own words for two or more of these words. As a class, research the dictionary definition for each word and compare it to the ones students have written.

Being Guided by Guide Words

There are two guide words at the top of each print dictionary page: the guide word on the left shows what the first word on the page is; the guide word on the right shows what the last word on the page is. The words on each page are words that come between the guide words. Example: The guide words on one page of a dictionary are *planet* and *platypus*. If you are looking for the word *plasma* or *platinum*, you know it will be on that page. The word *plague* will be on the preceding page and the word *please* will be on the next page.

Students can
- Turn to any page and identify the two guide words
- List three words that come between the two guide words
- Write the definition for one of the guide words
- List the word that appears directly after the first guide word; directly before the last guide word
- Find the page that the word *definition* appears on. What are the two guide words on that page?

Exploring an Online Dictionary

There are several online dictionaries available to students who need to find the meaning, spelling, and usage of a word. The Oxford Online Dictionary and the Merriam-Webster Dictionary are the most common references for students to investigate. For specific searches, the Internet provides reference for synonyms (e.g., The Macmillan Thesaurus), rhymes (The Rhyming Dictionary), and idioms (The Idiom Dictionary). Other examples of online dictionaries with specific content:
- Etymology Dictionary (word origins)
- Pseudodictionary (made-up words)
- Linguee, Ultralingua, Websters Online Dictionary: Rosetta Edition (multilingual dictionaries)

Students who are comfortable using the Internet to gather information will likely be comfortable looking up the definition of a word as needed. It is important that they also come to know many uses an online dictionary can have to help them inspect words. The most common searches are likely to include a word's

- definition
- usage
- correct spelling
- origin
- plural
- sample sentences

Teaching Tip

To help students understand what a dictionary can offer, it is best to give an example and demonstrate the features used by online dictionaries to support students when reading and writing. Display the definition of a word on an interactive whiteboard or have students investigate the word online to help them determine what an online definition of a word can include.

Going on a Word Hunt

Students work independently or with a partner to answer questions that give them practice in using dictionaries online; see Word Hunt on page 33.

Becoming a Dictionary Editor

This activity appears as Finding a Definition of Bullying in *Take Me to Your Readers* by Larry Swartz, pages 135–137.

What might the dictionary definitions be for each of these words?

bully, peace, friendship, education, technology

This activity guides students through the process of defining a word as they work independently, in pairs, in small groups, and as a whole class.

1. Introduce the activity by explaining to students that they are going to be lexicographers (those who write definition of words).
2. To begin, students work independently. Each student is given a file card on which to write a definition of a word; for example, they will define *bully* as a noun or as a verb. There is no restriction to word length.
3. Students pair off and exchange definitions. Ask each student to consider this question: What words or phrases from your partner's definitions do you think you might like to borrow to include in your definition? These suggestions could be recorded on a chart displayed to the whole class.
4. Pairs work together to synthesize definitions. Encourage students to include words from each partner's definition, perhaps adding words that have been listed on the chart.

Extension: Students examine definitions from a dictionary or the Internet to compare with their own.

5. Partners are matched with others to share definitions. In groups of four, students collaborate on a definition. Challenge students by insisting that the new definition be exactly 24 (or any other number of your choice) words in length. Once definitions are completed, one member of each group shares the collaborative definition with the whole class.
6. Shared writing is used to arrive at a class definition of the word. Each suggestion that is offered is recorded. The definition as revised and edited as the composing process unfolds.
7. Inform students that the new dictionary will be strictly visual, so all definitions must be represented without words. Prompt students to create an image or design to represent the word.

Vocabulary Skills Test

Circle a), b), or c) for each of the following vocabulary words. Can you get a perfect score? Once you are done, use the Internet or the dictionary to find out the meaning of the vocabulary words for each question.

1. The language origin of the word **ketchup** is…
   a) Spanish
   b) French
   c) Chinese

2. **Vuvuzela** is…
   a) a place name in South America
   b) a musical instrument
   c) a type of fabric used to make coats

3. The plural of the word **Sphinx** is…
   a) Sphinxes
   b) Sphinges
   c) Sphinxises

4. **Vichyssoise** is a…
   a) potato soup
   b) healthy juice drink
   c) French dessert

5. **Apatite** is…
   a) vegetable
   b) animal
   c) mineral

6. **Carombola** is…
   a) a fruit
   b) a dance
   c) a hat

7. A **boater**…
   a) steers a ship
   b) covers your head
   c) neither a) nor b)

8. An **awl** is…
   a) a math term used to describe quantity
   b) a carpenter's tool
   c) a part found in a car engine

9. What do you do with a **boobam**?
   a) eat it
   b) wear it
   c) play it

10. A **triolet** is…
    a) a type of poem
    b) a type of dance
    c) a mathematical term

11. An **armlet** is…
    a) a piece of jewelry
    b) a piece of medical equipment
    c) the area below your elbow

12. Which of these is not a dance?
    a) samba
    b) salsa
    c) shallot

13. Where would you most likely find a **sphygmomanometer**?
    a) a hospital
    b) a spaceship
    c) an orchestra

14. Where would you find a **divider**?
    a) a prison
    b) a football field
    c) a math class

15. **Pharynx** is…
    a) an Egyptian statue
    b) found in the body
    c) a city in the Middle East

Pembroke Publishers ©2019 *Word by Word* by Larry Swartz ISBN 978-1-55138-338-5

Word Hunt

1. List two definitions of the word *pie* in the online Oxford Dictionary.

2. In what part of the body can the **hippocampus** be found?

3. Use the online Macmillan Thesaurus to write three words that are synonyms for **sublime**.

4. List two three-syllable words found in the rhyming dictionary that rhyme with the word **syllable**.

5. a) Write the definition of the word **etymology**.

   b) What is the etymology of the word **etymology**?

6. What is the origin of the word **pomegranate**?

7. What is today's word of the day from any online dictionary? Write the definition of the word.

8. Write two sentences that are given to explain the meaning of the word **type** in the Merriam-Webster online dictionary.

9. a) What is the first word listed in the online Oxford Dictionary?

   b) What is the last word listed in the online Oxford Dictionary?

10. A group of giraffes is called a _____.

11. How does the online definition of the word **dictionary** explain how to pronounce the word?

12. Using the online Idiom Dictionary, find three idioms that feature the word **time**.

13. Write two plural forms of the word **cactus**.

14. What are three new three-syllable words added to the online Oxford Dictionary last year?

BONUS: Write a question about any vocabulary word for a friend to answer by going online.

Pembroke Publishers ©2019 *Word by Word* by Larry Swartz ISBN 978-1-55138-338-5

3

Does Spelling Count?

If I practiced
spelling words
in English
like saying them in Spanish
like—pehn-seel
for pencil,
imagine
— from *Imagine* by Juan Felipe Herrera; illus. Lauren Castillo

The aim of spelling learners, whether children or adults, is to discover the patterns that are there for them to find—and to use and to build words they might next need in their writing. Displaying lists of words and encouraging students to create their own lists helps stretch student investigation and understanding of spelling patterns.

In the introduction to her resource *The Spelling Teacher's Book of Lists*, spelling guru Jo Phenix explains:

> Making lists of words which share some element of spelling is a good idea. The act of making lists helps us to focus on the patterns. Once we have done this we will notice other words and can add to our lists. Seeing words grouped together can often help us to remember that they are similar. The lists can become a resource to use for checking spellings. (Phenix, 2003, p. 7)

Working with words helps students become aware of a particular pattern, noticing words that fit and words that do not fit. After they have focused on a particular pattern, students may find words jumping off the page, triggering a memory of similar words they have looked at before. A spelling pattern cannot be generalized from a few words. The more words we have, the more likely you are to spot the connections. The more we spot the connections, the better we are at recognizing, understanding, and applying our word-building skills.

Doreen Scott-Dunne effectively summarizes the goals of effective spelling practice:

> For students to become successful spellers, it is necessary for us to strike a balance between their inquiries into word patterns and their growing word knowledge. Key to that balance is that information from investigations and word knowledge is cognitively stored, easily and often accessed, and directly applied to proofreading and editing. By teaching spelling through inquiry and through having students pay attention to how words work, we can enable our students to become proficient spellers and engaged problem solvers with words. (Scott-Dunne, 2013, p. 124)

In this chapter, students will have opportunities to
- develop spelling power by focusing on patterns: vowels, consonants, syllables, prefixes, suffixes, root words, plurals, compound words, hyphenated words
- come to understand that effective spelling is a problem-solving process that uses knowledge of sounds, patterns, letters, and meaning
- use personal dictionaries as a reference to document familiar and unfamiliar words
- practice word building through independent and small-group activities
- become word detectives, strengthening their word knowledge by noticing, inquiring, and gaining information about words and how they are spelled
- build and use words they might need in their writing
- consider memory tricks (mnemonics) to reinforce spelling rules
- consider the strengths and challenges of participating in spelling bees

When we introduce building word strategies in our classrooms by focusing on patterns, we are helping students to build their understanding of how words work, so that they can expand their curiosity about words and apply this information in their writing.

Strategies that Help Us Grow as Spellers

- Look for patterns.
- Look for word parts.
- Write sounds in words that you know.
- Write a vowel in each word.
- Write a vowel in each syllable.
- Write the beginning of a word that you are sure of.
- Write the ending of the word that you are sure of.
- Think about words that sound the same.
- Think about the meaning of the word.
- Think of a rule that helps you remember the word.
- Use a dictionary or internet to check spellings.
- Ask someone for help.

(Booth & Swartz, 2004, p. 88)

Sound Patterns: Vowels

Teaching Tips

- An effective way to help students learn about vowels is to collect rhyming words that share the same pattern. Focusing on one spelling pattern can make it easier for students to make the connection between the sound and the letter(s) used to represent the sound.
- Generally, short vowels are easier to learn because the sounds are usually represented by one vowel only. Long-vowel sounds can be complicated because they usually consist of more than one vowel
- Investigating, collecting, and categorizing words can help students become aware of a spelling pattern (a sound and its spelling). Once students connect a sound with a letter or letters, they can make reasonable attempts to spell other words with the same sound.

Word-Building Activities with Vowels

Primary

1. Display a rhyming poem on a chart or interactive whiteboard. Read the poem out loud and then have students join in to chant the poem. Identify the rhyming pairs in the poem. Have students brainstorm other words that might have the same rhyme pattern.

   Rain, rain go *away*
   Come again some other *day*.

2. Display the following fill-in-the-blank letter combinations.

   s_t   p_t   s_n
   h_t   g_t   f_n

   Have students write three three-letter words for each of the following. Each of the three words should have a different vowel; e.g., t_ p (tip, top, tap)
   Bonus: add one letter to the following to make a four-letter word:

wrd	tck
pll	1st
frn	sng

Junior/Intermediate

The vowel combination *ea* has both a long-e sound (*please*) and a short-e sound (*head*). Students work with a partner to brainstorm *ea* words in two columns. A time limit of five minutes might add to the challenge.

Extension: Some students brainstorm and list words with *ea* and words with *ee*; both make the long-e sound. A time limit of five minutes might add to the challenge. Which is the longer list?

Sound Patterns: Consonants

Teaching Tips

- Building rhyming families can help students hear differences in the sound of words.

The word *latchstring* holds more consonants in a row than any other English word: ltchstr (six consonants).

- Consonant combinations at the end of words are difficult to hear clearly (*fold, strict*) The letters *m* and *n* that appear with a vowel before certain consonants create a sound that might be difficult to distinguish. When students leave out an *m* or *n*, they are likely not hearing the consonant sound; e.g., "stad" for *stand*, "cap" for *camp*.

Word-Building Activities with Consonants

Primary

1. Have students, in pairs, go on a word hunt in the classroom, examining posters, books, and signs. The challenge is to find and list ten words that begin with a two-consonant combination: e.g., *blue, friend, what*.

Extension

The activity can be repeated, having students investigate words that
- end in two consonants: e.g., *shrimp, kept*
- have three consonants in a row anywhere in the word: e.g., *string, weight*
- have double consonants; e.g., *tall, classroom*

Bonus

Students hunt for words that begin with two consonants and end in two consonants: e.g., *thing, thumb, spill*.

2. Present this string of words to the students:

   shoreshineshapefishcrashfinishovelleashshirtshellshoresharkshieldshop-
   shareshelvesharp

   There are no spaces between each word; they begin or end with *sh*. Have students write the separate words that appear in this puzzle (there are more than 15 words).

Extension

Students can create their own string puzzle using the consonant combinations *ch* or *th*.

Junior/Intermediate

Working alone or with a partner, students select any one page of the novel they are reading to go on a treasure hunt to find consonant words:
- Words that begin and end with two consonants
- Words that have three or more consonants in a row
- Words with double consonants
- Five-letter words with only one vowel
- Plural words with at least three different consonants

Syllables

Teaching Tips

- A knowledge of syllables can help students to spell. If they are aware of all the syllables or beats in a word, they can try to represent each beat or

This activity can be used for Intermediate students as well.

syllable with letters. Syllables allow students to work with smaller bits of information to which they can apply spelling strategies, such as phonic patterns and meaning patterns.

- Remind students that every beat contains at least one vowel.
- In order to demonstrate that syllables are linked to beat, clap out the beats of the words. Clapping the beats of familiar names will help students recognize one-syllable, two-syllable, and multi-syllable names.
- When students have difficulties with spelling multi-syllabic words, they may not be clearly enunciating the syllables in the words. Learning the strategy of saying words clearly in syllables can help students acquire new techniques for spelling development.
- Are students trying to represent every syllable in their written work? If parts of a word are left out, ask students to say the word out loud and listen for the beats. Students can then be encouraged to spell every beat. Clapping the beats can help them discover the number of syllables a word might have.

Word-Building Activities with Syllables

Primary

1. Read aloud a favorite nursery rhyme to the students. Repeat the activity, clapping the beats of each syllable. Students then join in to clap the beats/syllables of the poem as they say the words. As a final activity, students clap the beats only, without saying the words.

2. Arrange students into four groups according to the syllables in their first names: Group #1 (one syllable); Group #2 (two syllables), Group #3 (three syllables) Group #4, (four syllables or more). Which group is the largest? Point to students in each group and have them say their name and clap the syllable beats that accompany their name. The activity can be repeated using last names.

Junior/Intermediate

Invite students to brainstorm and list words on a chart according to the number of syllables in each word. For this activity, students can focus on a particular spelling pattern (e.g., words that end in the suffix –tion, words that end in the suffix –ment, words that begin with the prefix pre–). One-syllable words can be excluded from this chart.

Prefixes

Teaching Tip

- Two essential points for students to consider about prefixes:
    1. Their meaning: a prefix changes the meaning of the word it is added to.
    2. Their spelling: a prefix is always spelled the same way.

Word-Building Activities with Prefixes

Primary

Play a prefix game with the students: give clues to words that begin with a prefix; record answers as students suggest them. Then, review the words and circle the prefix in each word:

Prefix *bi*–: I am something with two wheels that you can ride. (bicycle)
Prefix *tri*–: I am a geometric shape with three sides. (triangle)
Prefix *sub*–: I am a ship that travels underwater. (submarine)
Prefix *un*–: I am the opposite of fortunately. (unfortunately)
Prefix *tele*–: TV is an abbreviation for the word. (television)
Prefix *trans*–: A bus, a car, a boat, a train are types of… (transportation).
Prefix *photo*–: This is a kind of picture I keep in a picture frame. (photograph)
Prefix *re*–: I do this to garbage to help save the environment. (reduce/reuse/recycle)

Junior/Intermediate

Provide lists of the common prefixes the students are likely to meet in their reading and writing. Students can work with one or two friends and discuss each of these prefixes, brainstorming other words that can be used as an example for each.

Prefix	Meaning	Example
auto–	self	autograph
extra–	outside	extraordinary
pre–	before	preview
re–	back, again	recycle, re-use
sub–	under	subtract
tele–	far	telescope
trans–	across	transport
un–	not	unknown

Groups can choose one of the prefixes and prepare a written list of words that use that prefix.

Extension

This can become a game, with each person (or team) listing words in a certain time limit. Students are encouraged to consider two-syllable, three-syllable, and multi-syllable words. Once the lists are, players score points for every syllable in the words they have listed.

- *Un*–, meaning "not," is the most common prefix in the English language; it is used mostly for adjectives (*believable/unbelievable*; *aware/unaware*). By exploring this prefix, students will come to realize that *un*– means "not" and usually changes a word to its opposite meaning. Students can work in pairs to play a prefix game. Each player in turn suggests a word that begins with the prefix *un–*. The game continues until a player is stumped and can't provide a word.

- Prefixes can often be used to write the opposite of a word. For example, by adding the prefix *ir–* to *regular*, the word made is *irregular*. Adding *un–* to *selfish* forms the word *unselfish*. Provide students with a list of words. They create the opposite of the words by choosing and adding the prefix *in–*, *un–*, *ir–*, or *im–*.

possible	equal	safe
accessible	movable	sure
accurate	possible	spell
available	read	true
do	replaceable	wind
edible	responsible	fantasy

Suffixes

Teaching Tips

- Informing students about the suffixes can prepare them to use ones that they are familiar with. Knowing part of a word leads students to spell words correctly. This applies to suffixes (and prefixes) because the spelling never changes.
- The suffixes *–ed* and *–ing* change the part of speech or tense. Words ending in *–ed* can be confusing, as they can make three different sounds: "t" sound (walked, missed), "d" sound (washed, climbed), or "ed" sound (lifted, wanted). All are spelled with *–ed.*

Word-Building Activities with Suffixes

Primary

Most adverbs end in *–ly*. Have students change the following adjectives to adverbs by adding the suffix *–ly*.

slow	strong	strong
quiet	careful	kind
soft	quick	happy
patient	loud	real

Junior/Intermediate

1. Students can explore prefixes and suffices by connecting syllables to make new words. Have students choose one syllable from each column to create three-syllable words. Syllables can be used more than once.

Column 1	Column 2	Column 3
ad	di	sion
com	ver	tion

con	van	tize
	nec	tage
	pen	ture
	fes	sate
	cus	
	clu	
	mis	
	ven	
	ces	

2. Have students solve the following word problems to spell a word correctly. Reminder: when the last sound in a word is a *y* by itself, it is changed to an *i* before adding a suffix.

Example: funny + er = funnier

silly + er =   wise + ly =
employ + er =   safest - est + er =
steady + ing =   tasty + est =
try + ed =   hurried - ed + es =
lucky + ly =   lucky + ly =
foolish + ly =   unfortunately - ly =
easy + ly =

Root Words

Teaching Tips

- A knowledge of roots can help students understand how words are built and therefore how to spell them. Breaking a word down into its component parts can help students to spell a word piece by piece.
- When we add prefixes and suffixes to roots we are building derivations. This can be a useful spelling strategy since, in most cases, the spelling of the root does not change. There are some exceptions; e.g., pronounce/ pronunciation (the *o* is omitted).
- When students are unsure about how to spell a word, suggest other words that are built from the same root. These patterns often give information that is not clear from looking at only one word.

Word-Building Activities with Root Words

Primary

Explain to students that root words can be built from one or more parts. A plural, prefix, suffix, or verb ending can be added to a root to form a new word

The word *spell* is a root word for other words: *speller, spelling, spelled, misspell.*

Remind students that by adding *–ing*, *–ed*, *–er*, or *–s* to root words, they can make new words. Have students add endings to the following verb roots to make new words.

pack	sew
wash	mix
cook	play

Junior/Intermediate

1. Have students suggest at least one other word that uses each of the following root words:

decide	sign
graph	please
add	revise
multiply	vary
divide	form
muscular	

2. Explain to students that Latin has given us many root words. For example, the Latin word *act* (meaning "do") is the root word for *action*, *react*, *actor*. Have students complete the following chart by adding at least two more words drawn from the Latin root.

Latin	Meaning	Words
man	hand	manufacture, manipulate, manual, manuscript
fer	bring	transfer
min	small	minor
opt	best	optimum
ped	foot	pedal
port	carry	portable
urb	city	suburb

International Spellings

Some spellings change over time. People in England, Australia, and New Zealand usually use older spellings. In the United States, people usually use the newer spellings. In Canada, some people may spell a word in the British way and some in the American way; most spell some words like the British and some words like Americans. When reading books or emails, we become accustomed to spellings that we see most, whether or not we recognize that the publication comes from a different country. It is a good idea to be familiar with alternative ways of spelling, and accept the most common way certain words are spelled in your country.

American Spellings	British Spellings
center	centre
theater	theatre
program	programme
traveled	travelled
enroll	enrol
favorite	favourite
neighbor	neighbour
realize	realise
catalog	catalogue

Plurals

Teaching Tips

- There are many plural words that don't seem to follow any pattern. When using these words in their writing, students can learn the irregular plurals as sight words.
- To address misspelled plurals in student writing, notice which spelling pattern the student does not understand. Working with students to develop a list of words that follow the same spelling pattern can help them become more familiar with forming plural words.

Word-Building Activities with Plurals

Primary

This activity can be simplified by omitting the words ending in *y*.

Have students prepare a shopping list by writing the plural form of each of these items.

egg	carrot	candy
apple	cookie	potato
pea	pie	french fry
peach	muffin	chocolate cake

Junior/Intermediate

Challenge students to correct the spellings of each of these plural words:

storys	taxies
mouses	cactus
witneses	hoof
familys	tomatos
womin	hippopatumuses
sheeps	busses
radices	serie's
mysterys	suffixs

Compound Words

Teaching Tips

Compound words should not be confused with portmanteau words, which are created when two words are joined and some letters or parts of a word (or both words) are dropped; e.g., *brunch*. See page 130 for more on portmanteau words.

- Beginning writers come to understand that they need to leave spaces between their written words. Most compound words are two words joined together and are written as one word.
- When joining two words together, the compound word does not drop any letters. Both words retain their spelling; e.g., *eggplant, bedtime, newsstand*.
- Knowing how to spell part of a compound word correctly can help with spelling of all other words using that part. For example, *somewhere, somebody*; *lighthouse, lightbulb*.

Word-Building Activities with Compound Words

Primary

Students make a compound word by joining two words together. Present the following list of words to students and challenge them to make ten or more words by joining two of them together. A word can be used more than once.

rain	basket	moon
ball	no	grand
every	ball	light
mother	any	beam
storm	park	bulb
where	bow	two

Junior/Intermediate

Create a compound word web with students that can be formed starting with a single word. Print the word (e.g., *land*) in a circle and then create a web around it, adding words that are compounds of the word; e.g., *landform, landfill, landscape, Iceland, homeland*. Suggested words for this activity include *ball, some, day, every, rain, town*. Students use the web to demonstrate how words are put together. Students work in pairs to brainstorm compound words. Or each partner can be assigned a word to make a word web. Which partner can list the most compound words in a set time limit (five minutes).

Hyphenated Words

Teaching Tips

- Two important rules—nay, commandments—of writing words with a hyphen:
    1. Hyphens mustn't be used interchangeably with dashes. This may not be problematic when handwriting, but it is important to teach students the difference between a hyphen and a dash on the keyboard. For example, note the difference between sugar-free and sugar–free.
    2. No spaces should be inserted around hyphens. For example, the word is sugar-free, not sugar - free.
- When looking up explanations for hyphenation on the Internet, we discover ten or more rules that need to be followed. Understanding and

I found this to be the case with apostrophes as well. When I attempted to teach my primary class the use of apostrophes, many children ended up using and abusing the apostrophe in their writing by liberally adding the punctuation mark to their writing.

applying these rules for elementary students can be overwhelming. In fact, when we invite students to use hyphens in their writing, students often overdo including them in their work. If students collect and inspect hyphenated words, they can come to recognize some patterns of usage that can lead them to apply their understanding when writing.

- It is worth pointing out, too, that compound hyphenated words eventually lose the hyphen over time. *Today*, *email*, and *ice cream* are examples (originally *to-day*, *e-mail*, *ice-cream*).

Using Hyphens: An Overview

Numbers: Hyphens should be used when writing numbers over twenty as words.

At the Ends of Lines: Hyphens are used to break words when they are broken over the end of a line of text. Tell students to break words between syllables. Students using the computer to write may need to hyphenate words in order to keep their margins flush or even.

Names: Some people have two names and choose to join them with a hyphen; e.g., Anne-Marie, John-Paul, Peggy-Sue. It's more common today to eliminate the hyphen. Many people choose to use one or more last names. In particular, many women choose to keep their maiden name and add the name of their spouse when they get married. They can choose to add a hyphen to their last names or not; e.g., Jasmine Hewitt-Smith, Lynda Bailey-Kerr.

Compound Adjectives: Hyphenated compound words are not as common as joined compound words. However, it is worth drawing students' attention to compound adjectives: two words joined together by a hyphen when they are placed before a noun. Point out to students, with examples, that the first of the two hyphenated words describes the other; both words do not describe the noun that comes after them.

> A *first-class* restaurant is not a *first* restaurant and it's not a *class* restaurant. It is a *first-class* restaurant.
> A *bad-hair* day is not a *bad* day or a *hair* day. It is a *bad-hair* day.

The title of the classic book by Herman Melville is *Moby-Dick,* but mention of the whale itself omits the hyphen (i.e., Moby Dick). The name Moby Dick was inspired by a real-life white whale known as Mocha Dick. The original title of Melville's book was *The Whale.* It was a copy editor who put the hyphen in Moby-Dick.

This activity can be used with Intermediate students as well.

Word-Building Activities with Hyphens

Primary

As part of their word-collecting culture, students can inspect and record hyphenated words encountered in newspapers, magazines, and books they are reading. Students can review whether these words are numbers, names, or adjectives.

Extension

Students might notice words that are hyphenated at the ends of lines. Have students explain why the hyphen appears in this part of the word.

Junior/Intermediate

1. These hyphenated word phrases were isolated from the novel *Secret Sisters of the Salty Sea* by Lynne Rae Perkins.

white-haired woman	long-ago grievances
ten-dollar bill	dried-up starfish
almost-best friend	flattened-out rabbit
sand-to-water mixture	old-fashioned furniture

   Have students identify the compound adjectives and nouns in each.

   Bonus phrases:

   itsy-bitsy gentle waves
   blue-and-white striped awning
   things-that-are-mostly-interesting-to-old-people mode

Extension

Have students choose any three of these phrases and write a sentence for each. As a further challenge, students add one adjective before each of the hyphenated adjectives.

2. Some compound words have more than one hyphen. Present groups of words with the order of the words scrambled up for students to unscramble and insert hyphens as needed; e.g. not me forget/forget-me-not.

   jack box the in
   me hand downs
   law mother in
   twenty old year
   earth to down
   not too ago long event
   ice cold cream ice cone

Mnemonics

Most people have demon words and puzzle over the proper spelling when writing those words. Mnemonics can help. Remembering how to spell *Mississippi* is now easy for me, as I recall the chant I learned in my childhood: "*M, I, double S, I, double S, I, double P, I.*" When I need to spell the word *accommodate*, I used to puzzle over the use of double consonants. Does the word have two c's and one m, or one c and two m's? I am reminded of this memory trick: Two cots and two mattresses went on a date (or two c's and two m's went on a date). To help my students spell the word *tomorrow* correctly, I broke the word down for them into three distinct words: *Tom or row*.

- *Mnemonic* is from the Greek and means "relating to memory." The Greek goddess of memory was known as Mnemosyne, which means remembrance.
- A mnemonic is a device, procedure, or operation that is used to improve memory. It is designed to tie new information closely to the learner's existing knowledge, making it easier to retrieve information. Spelling mnemonics are intended to help us remember the spelling of words.
- Some mnemonic clues help readers with tricky parts of the words. For example, when deciding which is correct, *arguement* or *argument*, remember: I lost an *e* in an argument.

- Some mnemonics help us differentiate different spellings, particularly with homonyms: Examples: (principal/principle) My princi*pal* is my *pal*; (hear/here) You h*ear* with your *ear*.
- Some mnemonics offer acrostic sentences providing a word for each letter of the sentence. For example, this mnemonic for the word *rhythm*:

> **R**hythm
> **H**elps
> **Y**our
> **T**wo
> **H**ips
> **M**ove

Here are some other mnemonic examples:
- **bookkeeper**: The word has three double letters: *oo kk ee*
- **because**: **B**ig **e**lephants **c**an **a**lways **u**nderstand **s**mall **e**lephants.
- **cemetery** is spelled with three e's: The lady screamed, "e-e-e" when she walked through the cemetery.
- **desert** or **dessert**: strawberry shortcake or sweet stuff reminds us to put two s's in the word dessert.
- **foreword**: The foreword of a book appears be*fore* the *word*.
- **separate**: There was a farmer named *Sep*; one day his wife saw a *rat* and yelled, "Sep, a rat—E!" As an alternative, you can remember that the words *para* and *rat* appear in the word.

Many students will have their own mnemonic rules for remembering how to spell words. Have them share their memory rules to help others with their spelling.

"Reading and writing are meaning-constructing activities but they are both dependent on words. All good readers and writers have a store of high-frequency words that they read and spell instantly and automatically." (Cunningham and Allington, 2016, p. 167)

In the Classroom: Personal Spelling Dictionaries
by Cassie J. Brownell, Grade 1 Teacher

On the opening day of school each year, a notecard sits on each child's desk. As they eagerly enter the room, I ask the children in my first-grade class to take up their pencils and, in their best handwriting, write the first letter of their first name in large print. Once they complete this, I distribute a thin-tip marker to each child and ask them to trace their names as they wrote them on the card. Collecting the cards, I then slip each name into the pocket-chart located on the wall for all to see. As a class, we then list the names of other important people and places we wish to display in the chart, such as the name of our school, the street our school is located on, the principal's name, and the city we all live in. The pocket-chart serves as a shared reference space for important words in our classroom and community that all children can access as they need when completing a writing task in class.

I then provide each child with a one-page document; it outlines various themes that could be personally relevant on the left side of the page and has a space for such words to be printed on the right side. For instance, the document lists words like *siblings* and *pets* on the left and has a blank to the right of it. We talk about how each person in class would have different words on their pages for most items, but that some of words may be the same, especially if we share "favorite foods" like pizza and ice cream. The children place these pages in their take-home folder, along with a short note to their caregivers that asks them to complete the page with their child and return it by the end of the week. Once completed, the children add this page to personal spelling dictionaries which they store in their desk to use as a reference point during both formal and informal writing lessons in class.

My Personal Dictionary

A — Addition, August, and, a, are, as, at, A Said, About, Altogether ★ PW all, am, an

B — brither, be, by, BeN, BEST, Blue, Brock, BecAUSe PW but

C — Count, CAT, cele·brate, community, coulj PW came, can, come

※ PW = Power Words - grade one

As the year continues, children add more words to their personal spelling dictionaries. For some, this means adding names of favorite sports heroes or characters from popular media. Other children, however, ask for assistance spelling verbs with spelling patterns they are not yet familiar with, such as "captured" or "journeyed," to make their stories more interesting. Likewise, using personal spelling dictionaries increases the confidence of the children and results in greater independence. As the year progresses, for example, I am not the only point of contact for children to add a word to their personal dictionaries. Instead, the children ask one another for assistance or, without missing a beat, call out that they could help their peer add that word as it was already in their dictionary.

The shared reference space in class as well as the children's personal spelling dictionaries serve as an individual reference point that encourage children to continue to write rather than getting hung up on a single word or phrase they do not know how to spell off the top of their head. In turn, the personal spelling dictionaries provide me insights as a teacher into the interests of my students as well as their understandings about word patterns.

To Bee or Not to Bee

Banananananananananana
I thought I'd win the spelling bee
And get right to the top,
But I started to spell "banana,"
And I didn't know when to stop.
— William Rossa Cole

A spelling bee is a competition in which contestants are asked to spell a wide selection of words, usually with varying degree of difficulty. Spelling bees can take place in the classroom, in the school community, or regionally and nationally. Rules vary according to the sponsorship of the competition, but generally words are pronounced according to the markings in the dictionary. The pronouncer gives the word and the dictionary definition. With the approval of the judges, the pronouncer may give a fuller explanation of the meaning of the word to supplement the dictionary definition. Contestants often ask for the word to be used in a sentence, to understand exactly what word is being presented and to buy time to think.

The spelling bee, by nature, is competitive. In an article considering competition written for the book *Creating Caring Classrooms*, teacher David Stocker argues,

> For decades, research has consistently condemned mutually exclusive goal attainment—where the success of one person or group depends on another's failure—and called into question the notion that competition in any form would be considered healthy. And yet in schools, intramurals and tournaments are pervasive, and the use of marks and grades are as entrenched as ever. (in Lundy & Swartz, 2011, p. 25.)

For those who suggest that a spelling bee provides an arena for those whose talents lie outside athletics (competitive sports), we perhaps need to invite them to consider what the true benefits are of competition, to consider who is being served in the classroom, community, or region, and what the learning and growth is for individuals who choose to embark on the practice. Building students' word power is significant and can be engaging (as this book suggests) and I would suggest alternative ways to enrich vocabulary and spelling knowledge (as this book presents).

There are many educators (myself included) who do not favor the classroom use of this program. Yet there are those who would argue that this "sport" has many benefits. In this list of strengths vs weaknesses, the *Nay*s outweigh the *Yay*s.

The Potential of Learning About Words through Spelling Bees

YAY

- Brings attention to students learning about words and spelling words correctly
- Provides an arena for those proficient in spelling to parade their knowledge
- Encourages some students to inspect and learn lists and lists of words
- Is universal

NAY

- Encourages rote memorization (which can be considered the least useful way to learn something)
- Can potentially humiliate (embarrass or stress) individuals who make an error and are eliminated
- Privileges competition as a way of learning at the expense of cooperation
- Ignites the tension and stress many participants experience when preparing for the spelling bee and being on stage
- Addresses a select few in the classroom who are proficient spellers
- Is not an inclusive activity that provides success for all learners in the classroom
- Predominantly centres on the individual rather than representing a collaborative, interactive mode of learning
- Teaches words without meaningful application
- Uses words that will not be used in everyday contexts or even outside of the competition (e.g., *gesellschaft, feuilletor*)
- Invites devout bee entrants to study (memorize?) words that can be found on The Consolidated Word List website. There are currently more than 24 000 words listed.
- Are oral, when spelling is best learned by seeing the word on the page in written form
- Provides no room for error or for learning from our errors. For example, having started to spell a word, a contestant may stop and start over, retracing the spelling of the words, but there can be no change of letters and their sequence from those first pronounced.
- Is centred on right or wrong answers; does not promote divergent thinking.

Alternative Activities to Spelling Bees

Bee for Two

This game is a spelling bee for two players. Each player is given a different list of ten words that are equally difficult. Two points are given for each correct spelling. Player 1 begins by calling a word to the opponent, challenging them to spell the word correctly. Players take turns calling out a word from their lists. When all twenty words have been completed, the duelists exchange lists and the game is repeated. This time one point is given for each correct spelling, with the goal being for both players to spell all twenty words correctly. The game can be made more challenging by making the lists longer, or by including more difficult words.

Novel Words

Students work in small groups of four or five, each with a novel in hand. Player 1 is the word caller and begins by announcing a word to the player to their right. That person attempts to spell the word correctly and, if they do so, receives two points. If not, the word is passed to the person on their right, who receives one point if correct; if that person is incorrect, the word caller informs the group of the correct spelling. The player who spells the word correctly continues the game by offering a word from his or her novel.

4

The Write Word

Heather Smith spent much of her early life wrestling with words. Not only was she a reluctant reader, she struggled with speech as well. Unable to pronounce certain words she became a walking thesaurus, anxiously swapping out words she wanted to say with words she could say. Although Heather's relationship with words was rocky, the two were eventually able to get over their difficulties and have been on speaking terms ever since.

Today, Heather wrestles with words in a different way—she is a writer! Instead of dodging them, she grabs them tight with both hands and finds them a home on the page.

— from an online biography of Heather Smith, author of *Baygirl, The Agony of Bun O'Keefe, Ebb & Flow*

Writing is thought on paper or screen. Words are the ingredients to make those thoughts visible. Writing is a complex act, a symbolic system—a means of representing thoughts, concepts, and feelings. When we write, we are digging into our memories and our mind dictionaries, ordering symbols to record our thoughts or communicate to others.

Making a shopping list draws on words we need to put down in order to buy the right thing—the write thing. When sending a greeting or condolence card to someone, we may pause and think carefully about the best way to express our feelings through words. Texting or sending emails usually involves a more spontaneous process when telling (or retelling) events, giving information, asking questions, or replying to questions we have been asked. When writing a poem, a ghost story, a persuasive letter, a report for science or social studies, students need to edit and revise their written work; this process demands emphatic attention, especially when handing in reports or essays, or completing a thesis when in university. And as I write this paragraph, I am continuously changing words, rearranging words, deleting words to ensure that my writing is clear and informative as an introduction to this chapter on writing. And am grateful for an editing process through which I will continue to refine these words before publication.

Writing cannot happen without words. It is a creative process that involves arranging and rearranging words, selecting and rejecting words, jiggling and juggling words. The more words students come to know, the wider the net for words to choose carefully in their writing and the deeper their understanding can be of the power of the word. In this chapter, students will have opportunities to

- use a word wall as a visual reference for site words and new vocabulary
- experience word sorting activities to notice patterns in words
- use personal word banks to collect words that can be used in their writing
- create a semantic map to consider words related to other words or a concept
- consider the use of synonyms to enrich their writing
- practice pattern writing that allows them to choose words carefully
- understand how revising our writing invites us to choose words to clearly express thoughts and ideas

Using Word Walls

A word wall—a visual display of words students have learned—acts as an immediate and accessible class dictionary and aids in the assimilation of high-frequency words. Word walls should always be used to associate meaning with practice activities: frequently used words should ultimately be automatic, not phonetically spelled, so that students can spend their time and energy decoding and understanding less-frequently used words. It is important, too, to draw their attention to the word wall and provide demonstrations on how to refer to the wall as needed.

Tips for Implementing Word Walls

- Words selected for a wall are those students commonly misspell, confuse with other words, or need often in their reading and writing.
- Five words per week can be added to a classroom word wall, usually on Monday, so the wall will comprise 200–250 words by the end of the year.
- Words can be displayed alone, with a picture, or with a sentence clue.
- Words are arranged alphabetically, preferably on different-colored pieces of paper, or written in different-colored markers, to help students easily differentiate the words and associate words and colors.
- In addition to adding new words to the wall, students can read and write those words each day.
- Word walls for older students can include words related to current events or topics they are studying in various curriculum areas (e.g., *pyramid*, *hieroglyphics*). In this context, word walls can resemble word webs, as words relating to shared topics are linked.

Word wall activities include
- Adding endings (e.g., *–s*, *–ed*, *–ing*) to words on the wall
- Handwriting practice
- Using the first letter to select a word that makes the most sense
- Making sentences from wall words

- Mind Reading: the teacher thinks of a word and gives the class clues to find the word
- Ruler Tapping: the teacher calls out a word and then taps out some of the letters without saying them or finishing the word; the students finish spelling the word aloud
- Sorting words based on features; e.g., all words ending in *t*; words that begin with a vowel.

Though the most common ways to display word-wall vocabulary is in alphabetical order, with words organized into each section, there are other ways words can be classified:
- double letters; e.g., *puppy, daddy*
- letter clusters; e.g., *–tion, –ish*
- compound words; e.g., *goldfish, housecoat*
- unusual letter clusters; e.g., *aardvark, vacuum*
- prefixes; e.g., *in–, de–*
- suffixes; e.g., *-tion*
- root words
- number of letters in the word
- rhyming words; e.g., *dear/fear/near*
- homophones
- plurals: regular and irregular
- contractions
- abbreviations
- synonyms
- antonyms
- functions
- proper nouns (including names)
- anagrams
- words that
  – begin and/or end with the same letter
  – rhyme
  – have the same vowel sound
  – describe the same theme or topic
  – have the same number of syllables
  – share a pattern; e.g., consonant or vowel in the initial, medial, or final position
  – contain smaller words when letters are left in order
  – contain silent letters

Word Sorting

For younger students, provide a list of categories for students to sort 10–15 wall words: e.g., by syllables, by function, singular or plural, or by spelling pattern (one-vowel words, two-vowel words, three-vowel words).

For this activity, students are challenged to sort words into categories. Provide a list of 20–30 wall words for students to sort. This activity is best done collaboratively; they solve the problem of how they can sort words into groups according to a common element. Students will also need to consider how many categories (columns) they will use to sort words. Once students have sorted words, they should be prepared to justify their categories. Word sorting can be done as a prereading activity, with students sorting content-specific words they might encounter in the reading of a story, novel, or unit of curriculum study.

Here is an example of a word-sorting activity using words connected to *home*. This activity might be used to introduce a unit on habitat (science), community (social studies), immigration (history), or issues in novels centred on homelessness or refugees. Have students group the *home* words presented here into categories so the words in each category share common elements.

abode	street	split-level	edifice
shelter	burrow	ranch	hut
condominium	windows	dwelling	structure
bungalow	homeland	casa	base
apartment	local	cage	castle
house	lodging	retirement	architecture
habitat	quarters	doors	family
zoo	sanctuary	domestic	barn
cave	address	location	hotel
residence	roost	zip/postal code	floor
cottage	haunt	site	rooms
flat	digs	depot	ocean

Using Word Banks

Word banks give students ownership and investment in the words they learn, increasing their interest and enthusiasm for learning in general. Students choose key words from their reading based on a quality (e.g., sound, length), record the words on index cards, and file them in a personal word bank. Because students own their banks, they recognize their words more easily. The teacher may add complementary words to the bank to emphasize concepts (e.g., sound–letter relationships), but it is the students who ultimately control their banks and the words in them. Each student word bank may have two sections:
1. Words being learned, discovered
2. Recognized words

Words can be
- practiced
- matched
- shared
- traded
- used in posters
- illustrated
- discussed
- sorted
- cut and pasted
- expanded
- used to generate rhyming words

It is the students who ultimately control their banks and the words in them. David Booth suggests that they write words they know in a Life Words book, the words that will support their literacy lives: family names, food they like, sports heroes, favorite toys and TV shows. Soon they will have one hundred words they can recognize in print.

Semantic Mapping

Semantic mapping is a strategy that encourages students to consider a word or concept and its relation to other words and ideas. It is an instructional strategy that can be used with students in any grade to consider prior knowledge connected to a topic or as a way for students to synthesize information they have learned, a story they have listened to, or a novel they have read.

Teaching Tips

- Demonstrate semantic mapping by creating a semantic map with the whole class. As students offer suggestions connected to a topic, you can record them on a semantic map displayed on a chart or interactive whiteboard.
- To help younger students explore semantic mapping, offer them topics that use vocabulary they are familiar with.
- As students become familiar with the process, suggestions for branching items can be offered so they can expand and sort their thinking.

In Chapter 2 of her book *Making Words Stick*, author Kellie Buis provides background information, step-by-step instructions, and graphic organizers to use with this instructional strategy.

To begin, a word, phrase, event, theme, or issue is presented to students. In pairs or small groups, students brainstorm any concepts and related words that connect to the focus word. For example, younger students might consider the focus word *animals*. The word *animals* would appear as the focus word in the centre of the chart. Branches could extend from the chart to list the names of animals according to a given category: e.g., four-legged, two-legged, no-legged animals; or mammals, reptiles, sea creatures, and flying animals. Other possible topics include occupations, the four seasons, celebrations, emotions, things we read, etc. For older students, the semantic mapping strategy can help them reflect and respond to elements of a novel; e.g. character descriptions, setting, problems (conflicts).

With thanks to Cathy Marks Krpan.

In the Classroom: Semantic Mapping Math Words
by Anne Tony, Grade 5 Teacher

In my Grade 5 program, I often used semantic mapping to have students consider words and phrases connected to a particular theme or concept (e.g., words to describe a fictional character, words to comply with a spelling pattern). I decided to use this approach in a mathematics lesson in order to have the students consider terminology and ideas connected to geometry. When I told my students that we would be using semantic mapping in math, some of them were somewhat surprised, since they thought this was just a language strategy and did not see how it would be useful for math. I explained to them that language is everywhere. I stressed that we can use many of the strategies we use to learn language to learn math, because math is also a language. I stressed that, just like with a language semantic map, we would place a math word/concept in the middle of the page and think of different ideas and words that would connect to that word.

The goal of introducing semantic mapping was to engage students in exploring mathematical language and communicating their ideas through writing. I strongly believe that students need to become good communicators in all areas of the curriculum, including math. We know that students don't use outside the classroom most of the vocabulary they use in math class. I want to ensure that my students have an understanding of the math concepts and language they are learning and felt that this interactive, collaborative activity might help them better come to grips with the vocabulary of geometry.

As students began the semantic map for the concept of *congruent*, they immediately connected the word *same* and then connected the word shapes. After including those two words, they began to struggle a bit, as they were not sure of what else they could add. I decided to push their thinking forward by asking them to consider other ideas they knew about word *congruent* and the work we had done related to congruency in class. After some discussion, they began to connect words that described the attributes of shapes that are congruent, such as *angles* and *area*. Use of such words as *distance*, *visual*, and *equal* revealed their understanding of concepts. I noticed that one group connected the word *reflection* to the focus word, since congruent shapes are indeed reflections of each other. This was a new idea that we had not explored yet! I noticed that students did not include 3D shapes nor any words related to 3D shapes, such as *width* and *height*. This helped me to consider what the students know and what I might introduced to further their understanding. Moving forward, I hoped to include more examples of 3D shapes in my teaching as well as rich descriptives to describe them.

The students felt that this activity, while a bit challenging at times, enabled them to think about all the words and ideas they could use to describe math and communicate their ideas. What I appreciated was the rich talk related to mathematics that this activity facilitated as students created their maps and exchanged ideas. When groups shared their maps with other groups, it was interesting for them to identify and compare the different connections and words used by others.

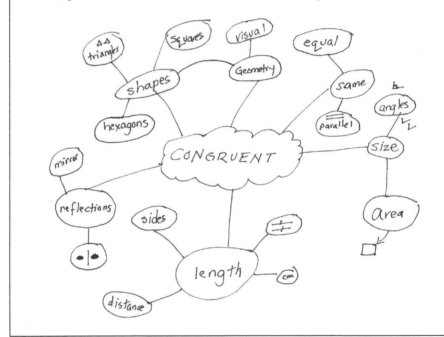

Making Word Connections

A nucleus word is put in the centre of a chart. Key words are radiated outwards from the nucleus word. Further lines radiate out from the key words and meanings are listed.

Exploring Synonyms

The word *synonym* is from the Greek word *synonymon*, which refers to words having the same sense as another. The origin of the word *origin* is the Latin word *originem*, which means a rise, commencement, beginning, or source. These words are synonyms for the word *origin*: *ancestry, element, motive, causality, derivation, generator, impulse, inception, inspiration, nucleus, progenitor, provenance, seed, wellspring, horse's mouth.*

One way to help students organize words is to have them consider words that have a similar meaning (synonyms) or opposite meanings (antonyms). When looking up a definition of word, the online dictionary often provides synonyms and antonyms for most words. Drawing attention to synonyms and antonyms further increases students' word power since it encourages them to make connections and consider associations between one or more words and develops their vocabulary prowess.

Using a Thesaurus

The picture book *The Right Word: Roget and His Thesaurus* by Jen Bryant and Melissa Sweet celebrates the life of Peter Mark Roget and provides information of how he came to publish the thesaurus in 1852.

When writing, students should also become familiar with using a thesaurus to replace words that may be bland or redundant, or to find a word to better express what they are trying to say. Students should be encouraged to use a thesaurus when they are revising their writing and looking at the words and language they have used. In fact, they can be invited to read through their own piece of writing and identify two or three words that they feel might be improved on; then they could select replacements from those offered in the thesaurus. In some ways, the thesaurus is the opposite of a dictionary, since students need to have a meaning already. Sometimes a synonym might have a slightly different meaning from the intended use; however, when given a choice of vocabulary, writers can decide which word best suits their creative need.

Teaching Tips
- Many spellcheckers identify unknown words and suggest possible alternatives from which the students might choose.
- It is important to point out to students that some words have more than one meaning and a dictionary might offer synonyms for each definition. For example, one definition of the word *ground* is "the solid part of the earth's surface" and suggested synonyms are *globe, mainland, floor, archipelago, earth, soil*; for the definition of *ground* as "a rational motive or belief," suggested synonyms include *account, occasion, reason, score.*

Using a Dictionary

To help students understand that a single word can have several synonyms, choose and display a word (e.g., *identity*) and ask students to suggest alternatives. Then have students use a print or online dictionary or thesaurus to investigate synonyms for the word *identity*: *character, integrity, ipseity, name, personality, singularity, selfdom, status, uniqueness*. Ask students to identify any synonyms that they might not be familiar with. Which word on the list might they choose to use in their own writing? Which synonyms are particular to describing specific things?

Extension

Students can work independently to investigate and list synonyms for any two of the following adjectives:

beautiful	nice
neat	creative
happy	smart
clean	scary

Which word has the most synonyms? Which synonym is unusual/unfamiliar? Which synonym(s) might you use in your own writing?

Replacing Words

Have students examine an excerpt from a novel they are reading. Students focus on two or three words from the passage and investigate synonyms that might be considered for replacing those words. Students can rewrite the passage with the chosen synonyms.

Extension

How many synonyms can students suggest for the word *awesome*?

Students can go through a similar process by revisiting and revising a piece of their own written work.

Patterns for Writing

Patterns for writing present creative structures that order or arrange ideas into specific formats that provide signals for the reader. Providing students with many opportunities to hear and experiment with a potpourri of formats that are meaningful to their lives, to discuss both the distinctive and similar linguistic features of certain modes, and to share their own pieces of writing is significant to the development of young writers. When teachers read aloud strong examples of genres of writing, students can be inspired to create their own works and develop an understanding of how to write like a reader and read like a writer.

See pages 59–62 for suggestions for writing poetry according to a formula.

This list provides just a glimpse of some forms of writing:

advertisements	narratives
alphabet books	nursery rhymes
brochures	opinions
commercials	poetry
descriptive paragraphs	posters
fables	questionnaires
graphic texts	recounts
interviews	reports
job applications	scripts
letters	spoken-word poems
lists	verses

Mentor texts, genres, formats, and shapes offer supportive structures for writing down thoughts and feelings. David Booth explains, "We hitch-hike along with the writers and artists who motivated us into action, taking off from their initial creations but making the work our own" (Booth, 2016, p. 84). These samples of student writing demonstrate how students have "borrowed" syntactic patterns from picture books to create their own pieces of writing.

Pattern 1

Source: *Somewhere Today: A book of peace* by Shelley Moore Thomas; photographs Eric Futran

Syntactic pattern:

Somewhere today… someone is learning to do things in a different way.
Somewhere today… someone is planting a tree where one was cut down.

Grade 2 student samples:

Somewhere in the school is a girl named Rika writing a sentence.
Somewhere today... there is a mystical land where a gryphon is chasing a flysnake.
Somewhere today... there are clouds making shapes in the blue sky.

Pattern 2

Source: *Reading Makes You Feel Good* by Todd Parr
Syntactic pattern:

Reading makes you feel good because… you can travel to faraway places.
Reading makes you feel good because… you can follow signs on the road.

Grade 1 student samples:

Reading makes you feel good because… you can imagine you are a king in a castle.
Reading makes you feel good because… we can learn about make-believe stories and be smarter.

Pattern 3

Source: *Sometimes I Feel Like A Fox* by Danielle Daniel
Syntactic pattern:

Sometimes I feel like a fox,
Sly and sharp.
I observe all those around me
And disappear quickly.

Grade 4 student sample:

Sometimes I feel like a raven.
Sneaky and mysterious.
I can fly high as an eagle
And can keep the secrets that you tell.

Bookshelf: Picture Book Sources for Patterning

John Burningham. *Would You Rather…*
Danielle Daniel. *Sometimes I Feel Like a Fox* (also *Once in a Blue Moon*)
Drew Daywalt; illus. Oliver Jeffers. *The Day the Crayons Quit*
Rebecca Kai Dotlich; illus. Fred Koehler. *One Day: Short, very short, shorter-than-ever stories*
Wendy Ewald. *The Best Part of Me*
Jennifer McGrath; illus. Josée Bisaillon. *The Snow Knows*
Karen Kaufman Orloff; illus. David Catrow. *I Wanna Iguana*
Todd Parr. *Reading Makes You Feel Good* (also *The Peace Book*; *The Thankful Book*)
Shelley Moore Thomas; photo. Eric Futran. *Somewhere Today: A book of peace*

List Poem Activities

Writing list poems by preparing a list of words with a specific topic provides an ideal pattern for students to brainstorm and present ideas. Sometimes list poems feature one word per line. The title of a list poem readily suggests the topic that is being presented. Some list poems feature more than one word and might follow a particular rhyme scheme.

Writing an I Like… List Poem

Margaret Wise Brown has a delightful list poem "I Like Apples," in which she presents a list of the kinds of apples she likes, repeating the word *apples* on every line. Her list includes *Red apples, Green apples, Whole apples, Half apples*. This poet's words have inspired me to write the following list poem:

I Like Words
    by Larry Swartz
I like…
old words
new words
lost words
found words
silly words
strange words
plain words
fancy words
peculiar words
particular words
humdrum words
awesome words
scrumdiddlyumptious words
Jabberwockdelicious words
book words
song words
my words
your words
words collected, words inspected
Yes, I really do like words!

Young children can aptly create their own poem on a topic of choice by following this pattern. The topic of the poem appears at the end of each line; e.g., dogs, cars, candy, toys, books, flowers, fruit, etc.). In each line, an adjective is given to describe the noun. For young children, it is best to give a template and model how to write a list poem using the pattern in the margin.

List poem pattern:
I like _____
_____ _____
_____ _____
_____ _____
_____ _____
Yes, I like _____

Writing a Favorite Words List Poem

In her book *Read! Read! Read!*, poet Amy Ludwig VanDerwater has presented a list poem entitled "Word Collection" in which she lists her favorite words, including "Knickknack," "Pickpocket," "Alligator," and "Jumping Jack." Students can create their own poems by presenting a list of favorite words they have collected because of their look, their spelling, their sound, or their unique quality.

Extensions

- Students can use the computer to create a vertical list of collected words. For further creativity, different fonts can be used.
- Some students might challenge themselves to create a poem using rhyming couplets or an a/b/c/b rhyme scheme.

Working Inside and Outside a List Poem

Bird Is Word

by David Booth

Bird is Word
Hawk is eye,
Owl is stare,
Robin – spring,
Dove is pair.
Vulture – death,
Albatross – fear,
Crow is thief,
Seagull – pier.
Loon is laugh,
Cardinal – red,
Jay is blue,
Pigeon – bread.
Swan is glide,
Crane is leg,
Sparrow – flock,
Chicken – egg.
Turkey – farm,
Wren is small,
Hummingbird – wings,
Ostrich – tall.
For each bird,
Just one word,
One feathered thought –
The bird is heard.

Let's talk about the poem:

- Which birds in this poem have you seen?
- Why did the poet use hyphens in some lines and not others?
- What is the function of using a period on every fourth line?
- How accurate do you think each of the one word descriptors is for each bird?
- What process do you think David Booth used to create "Bird Is Word"?

Let's read the poem aloud:

- This poem can be read chorally in pairs, small groups, or the whole class with each student being assigned one line (or part of a line) of the poem.
- What gesture or action might students use to accompany the line of text said out loud?

Creating Visual Images

Students can create an illustration for one of the lines of this poem. The illustrations accompanied by the line of text can be transformed into a picture book or online presentation.

Inquiry

Students work in pairs, each pair assigned the name of bird in the poem. Students brainstorm facts that they know about the bird. Using information from nonfiction books or the Internet, students list additional facts about the bird.

Writing a List Poem

Students may use the pattern created by David Booth to create a list poem on a topic of their choice; e.g., My Classmates, A Sport, Dogs, Food. The list poem could be rhymed or not.

Revising and Editing Our Words

Teachers need to help students understand that revising and editing are important and essential processes to undertake when preparing a piece of writing for publication. Many students come to realize the need for editing, but spotting mistakes and omissions and revising ideas can be challenging. Students may be motivated to refine and polish their work and to put in an effort to make changes, add or eliminate ideas, and choose words carefully to effectively communicate their thoughts. Students often need help in knowing what to revise, and need specific ideas and strategies that will make their writing more effective. Teachers can work one-on-one with a student or offer a mini-lesson that highlights one aspect of the writer's craft.

The editing process has two elements:

1. Revising
2. Editing

Revision concerns content and begins when a writer has completed a first draft. Writers need to check their work and ask questions, such as *Is all the information included? Are there parts that are repetitive or stray from the topic? Is the information ordered logically?* All writers—students in our classroom, adults, professional authors—need to revise their work if it is going to be shared with others. In the classroom, students might find it helpful to have a partner read their work to see more readily areas that need to be improved. This editor's assessment of the work, along with the writer's own assessment, should lead to further drafts where adjustments can be made.

Editing is about correcting errors in spelling, grammar, and punctuation. The editing process helps students carefully inspect each word and consider if it is spelled correctly and used correctly. Too often too much time is spent on this when stronger effort needs to be put into larger issues such as narrative flow, clarity of expression, relevance of information—and word choice!

Teaching Tips

- Dictionaries, thesauruses, word games, and literature should be available to support students in the revision process.
- Remind students that refining and polishing their work is essential if it is going to be shared with an audience; e.g., classmates, teacher, school community, families.

Focusing on Words for Revising and Editing: Ten Suggestions

As students collect words and expand their word knowledge, they are perhaps better prepared to make good word choices in their writing. Have them consider the following:

1. Use strong verbs, effective adjectives and adverbs.
2. Look up synonyms for a word in a thesaurus.
3. Replace overused words; e.g., *nice, said, a lot.*

4. Use an unusual word you have discovered.
5. Use word banks and personal dictionaries.
6. Use metaphor or simile effectively.
7. Show, rather than tell, by describing actions and events.
8. Consider strong word choices made by a favorite author.
9. Ask for assistance and recommendations from classmates.
10. Try not to be satisfied with the first word that flows from the pen, pencil, or keyboard.

Demonstration Lessons

See Replacing Words on page 58 and Triple-Scoop Words below for ideas.

1. Choose a sentence from the newspaper or a piece of fiction or nonfiction. Invite students to become editors and make three recommendations for changing or adding words to make the writing more effective. Focus could be on use of adjectives or adverbs.
2. From a student's portfolio (preferably from the previous year or from another class), select a piece of draft writing that needs editing and revising. Or create a piece of writing that demonstrates specific editing issues you want students to examine. Transcribe it onto a screen or make individual copies. In small groups, students can become editors and make suggestions for revisions. To model the editing process, incorporate student suggestions by crossing out, adding, and deleting information.

Many thanks go to Adrienne Gear for offering the following concept and for granting permission to use this material that appears in her two essential resources on teaching writing: *Writing Power* (page 49) and *Nonfiction Writing Power* (pages 38–39), both Pembroke Publishers.

In the Classroom: Triple-Scoop Words
by Adrienne Gear

There are approximately a quarter of a million words in the English—that's a lot of words to choose from! Artists spend a long time mixing colors until they find the right tone. Writers need to take time to find the right words, the best words to express themselves. If an artist used the same two colors all the time, the pictures might be boring to look at. If a writer used the same words over and over, the writing would be boring to read. Having a huge palette of words can help us become more colorful writers.

Whether writing fiction or nonfiction, choosing interesting and sophisticated words for our writing can enhance the quality of the work. I like to think about special words as "triple-scoop" words, comparing words to ice cream. A single scoop is okay but, let's face it, it's just a little lump of ice cream and often leaves you wishing you had more. Sometimes when reading student writing, I notice a lot of "little lump" words of description. These words leave me feeling somewhat unfulfilled. Our goal is to help students use triple-scoop words in their writing in order to make it more delicious and to make a reader feel more satisfied.

Single Scoop	Triple Scoop
sad	devastated, depressed
mad	furious, livid
good	amazing, fantastic

The following outline helps students to consider the use of triple-scoop words in both fiction and nonfiction writing.

- Demonstration: Write the following sentences on a chart or on an interactive whiteboard.

Fiction
My little sister bugs me a lot.
Annoying doesn't even begin to describe my pesty little sister.
Nonfiction
Most spiders make nice silk to make big webs for getting prey.
Most spiders make delicate strands to create sturdy webs for capturing prey.

Ask students which sentence is more interesting to read and why. Remind students: One of the goals of writing is to capture the interest of the reader. Using triple-scoop words instead of single words can help make the reader stay interested in what we have to say.

- Practice: Provide students with a list of words. Working with a partner or in groups of three, students can suggest three triple-scoop words for each item.

hot	small
wet	slow
lovely	nice
tired	beautiful
happy	said

- Teaching Tip: Display a triple-scoop word list in the classroom. The teacher, along with students can continue to add triple-scoop words as they encounter them in the books they read and in their word collecting experiences. Words can be displayed as ice-cream cone images. A single-scoop word is written on the cone and the cone is filled with scoops of ice-cream, each with a different triple-scoop word.

5

Reading the Words We Need

Lord Polonius: What do you read my lord?

Hamlet: Words, words, words.

Lord Polonius: What is the matter, my lord?

Hamlet: Between who?

Lord Polonius: I mean, the matter that you read, my lord.

— from William Shakespeare, *Hamlet*, Act II, Scene 2

"Words, words, words," is Hamlet's answer to Polonius's question, "What do you read, my lord?" Polonius wants to know the meaning of the words that Hamlet is engaged with, but in his three-word response, Hamlet suggests that words are meaningless, a medium for thoughts not actions. Hamlet seems to be saying that words are all we have, tools that can lead to making meaning.

Hooray for educator Janet Allen, who used Hamlet's answer for the title of her book *Words, Words, Words* about vocabulary teaching. Drawing on research from Nagy, Herman, and Anderson, Allen came to recognize that "reading is the single most important factor in increased word recognition" and that "reading is at the heart of a word-rich classroom." Like many teachers, Janet Allen began teaching vocabulary by asking students to look up words in a dictionary and write the words in sentences, and by giving weekly vocabulary tests. She realized that her students gained hardly enough in-depth knowledge from this practice to integrate the words in their spoken or written language. Upon reflection, Allen discovered that her secondary students needed extensive reading and direct instruction in word-learning strategies in order to become fluent independent readers (Allen, 1999, p. 10).

Award-winning Kate DiCamillo is one of my favorite authors for middle-years readers. A recent release, *Louisiana's Way Home* (2018), plucks a feisty character from DiCamillo's previously written novel *Raymie Nightingale* and tells the story of Louisiana Elefante's forced journey to Georgia, where she leaves behind her

Florida friendships and a place called home. In italics in the passages here are some words that I encountered and pondered over while reading this novel written predominantly for nine- to twelve-year olds:

> I had a sudden feeling of *irrevocableness*, and I thought *I have to get out of this car. I have to go back.* (p. 6)

> Because the curse of Granny's father is not a tooth curse. It is a curse of *sundering*. (p. 22)

> I applied the gas, and the car went roaring up the embankment onto the *macadam*. (p. 32)

> That's what they do all *ding-danging* day long. They like working on machinery. (p. 150)

> I looked into Reverend Obertask's sad *walrus* face. (p. 164)

Why these particular words? I used sentence clues to help me understand that *irrevocableness* was a noun that had something to do with needing to change what was happening. I skipped over the word *sundering* when it first appeared in the novel, but by the third time it made its appearance, I grabbed my smart phone to find its definition (i.e., split apart, divided). I did not, however, look up the word *macadam* (which I originally thought might be a palindrome) and realized that I didn't really need to know where Louisiana ended up driving the car. I loved the look and the onomatopoeic sound of the frivolous word *ding-danging*, ideal for describing work on machinery, and the choice of *walrus* perfectly painted a picture of this character.

As a fluent, adult reader, I would say that I recognized almost 100% of Kate DiCamillo's word choices. Pausing and thinking about the particular words helped me to think about not only about how masterful this author is at choosing and using vocabulary, but also how I made sense of text. I also considered how young readers would respond to the somewhat unusual words in the novel. These highlighted words may be added to my personal word repository, but I would likely need to meet—and use—any of these words a number of times in order for them to be deposited in the permanent word bank of my mind, what spelling guru, J. Richard Gentry calls the "dictionary in your brain."

Reading texts of all kinds exposes kids to more and more words, providing better background knowledge of vocabulary, word meanings, and word spellings. As readers develop, they have an increased ability to recognize words, and on the path to fluency they can develop strategies for processing unfamiliar words, which in turn helps deepen comprehension. Noticing new vocabulary, guessing at word meanings, investigating meanings, underlining, celebrating, and collecting words from all kinds of texts contribute to students' exponential growth in reading (and writing) and understanding of the words they need to do so successfully. In this chapter, students will have opportunities to

- Appreciate and respond to rich verbal text that appears in picture books (read aloud and independently)
- Develop word-solving strategies that help them to process meaning before, during, and after reading a text
- Appreciate rich verbal text found in novels and explore an author's style and language through response activities

- Consider how an author's words can effectively create pictures in the mind and appeal to the senses by examining snippets/fragments of language from picture books and novels
- Develop a fascination with words found in literature by collecting unfamiliar vocabulary, including invented language
- Expand their word knowledge by making meaning of special words encountered in the content areas

Sight Words

To read effectively, a reader has to recognize words quickly, accurately, and easily. Readers translate written symbols that are grouped into words in their oral representation, hearing them inside the head during silent reading. In order to focus on making meaning with the text, the reader has to become efficient at word recognition with as little effort as possible. Familiar words need to be recognized automatically; difficult words need to be recognized using a variety of techniques. Most of the words we learn to recognize almost subconsciously are learned as we read, where the context drives the reader toward making sense of the words as the reader is involved in authentic reading and construction activities. High-frequency words should not be taught as a separate category of words to be memorized, but should be taught as part of phonics, shared-reading, and guided-reading experiences.

Lists of basic sight words are useful because they tell us which words in our language are used most frequently. Charts of sight words can be displayed in the classroom, presented in a word wall or modified and presented to individual students. Sight-word lists can be prepared from words you observe your students writing frequently.

See page 68 for a list of 200 sight words from Booth and Swartz (2004) *Literacy Techniques*, p. 117.

- Dolch word lists provide the most commonly used words from pre-Kindergarten to Grade 3. The list of 315 words was devised by Dr. Edward William Dolch. A separate list of high frequency words has also been suggested. See http://www.sightwords.com/sight-words/dolch/#lists
- Fry Word Lists: Going beyond the Dolch lists, Dr. Edward Fry devised lists of the most common words used in reading and writing. His lists were introduced in 1950 and updated in 1980. The lists are presented in order of frequency—"instant words"— and are often broken down into groups of 100. Learning all 1000 of Fry's high-frequency words would equip a child to read books, newspapers, and websites.

Word-Solving

Word-study activities generally take place before or after the reading of the text:
- Before reading: We introduce key words and concepts, drawing attention to language concepts and special, necessary vocabulary.
- During reading: We guide each student to apply increasingly flexible word-solving strategies to negotiate unfamiliar words.
- After reading: We review and reinforce application of strategies, and introduce new letter patterns and structures.

The First Hundred Instant Words							
Words 1–25		**Words 26–50**		**Words 51–75**		**Words 76–100**	
the	on	or	can	will	make	number	its
of	are	one	said	up	like	no	now
and	as	had	there	other	him	way	find
a	with	by	use	about	into	could	long
to	his	word	an	out	time	people	down
in	they	but	each	many	has	my	day
is	I	not	which	then	look	than	did
you	at	what	she	them	two	first	get
that	be	all	so	these	more	water	come
it	this	were	how	so	write	been	made
he	have	wee	their	some	go	call	may
was	from	when	if	her	see	who	part
for		your		would		oil	
Common suffixes: -s, -ing, -ed, -er; -ly, -est							

Words from 100–200							
Words 101–125		**Words 126–150**		**Words 151–175**		**Words 176–200**	
over	give	say	same	set	here	try	point
new	most	great	tell	put	why	kind	page
sound	very	where	boy	end	ask	hand	letter
take	after	help	follow	does	went	picture	mother
only	thing	through	came	another	men	again	answer
little	our	much	want	well	read	change	found
work	just	before	show	large	need	off	study
know	name	line	also	must	land	play	still
place	good	right	around	big	different	spell	learn
year	sentence	too	form	even	home	air	should
live	man	mean	three	suck	us	away	Canada
me	think	old	small	because	move	animal	work
back		any		turn		house	
Common suffixes: -s, -ing, -ed, -er; -ly, -est.							

The main goal for word study is to provide students with strategies for independence. Fountas and Pinnell refer to the process of figuring out unfamiliar words as *word solving* because it involves a variety of strategies beyond simple decoding. It is recommended that we teach word-solving strategies one at a time, modeling them and providing opportunities for guided practice. Some teachers like to maintain classroom anchor charts to remind students of strategies they should try.

Instruction during guided reading is the most meaningful way to help students understand and use word-solving strategies. The guided-reading lesson focuses on developing confidence, fluency, independence, and early-reading strategies. Teachers need to be aware of each student's competencies, experiences, and interests. Teachers can guide and demonstrate how to make sense of unfamiliar or challenging words. The goal is to provide students with strategies that "good readers" use when they are reading independently.

Ten Tips for Word Solving

1. **Checking**: Check the picture to help you figure out the word.
2. **Chunking**: Can you recognize any letter chunks or patterns? Is there a familiar little word inside a big word?
3. **Cross-checking**: Use word walls and other classroom charts as a reference for solving words in texts.
4. **Stretching**: Stretch the sounds in the word; sound it out.
5. **Sliding**: Take a running start and slide right into the word.
6. **Monitoring**: Stop and think about whether the word makes sense, sounds right, and matches the print.
7. **Skipping**: Skip a hard word and read on; sometimes the rest of the sentence will help you with the word.
8. **Rereading**: Go back to the beginning of the sentence and start again.
9. **Fixing**: If you read a word that doesn't make sense, sound right, or look right, go back and fix it up.
10. **Guessing**: Guess what word might make sense in the sentence. See if the sounds in your guess match the letters on the page.

Appreciating Words in Picture Books

"Let the wild rumpus start!"
— from *Where The Wild Things Are* by Maurice Sendak

Max, the hero of Maurice Sendak's book *Where The Wild Things Are*, is called a "wild thing" by his unseen mother and sent to bed without supper. In the magical part of the story, Max discovers a land of real wild things, and leads them in a wild rumpus. "What's a rumpus?" a young reader might ask. In response, an adult sharing the book might ask the following questions: *What words like rumpus do you know? What in this the pictures help us to understand what a rumpus is? What's another word for rumpus?* Or better yet, the adult might remain silent and let the child figure it out for themself. *Rumpus* is a word that will likely never have been heard by children until they experience Sendak's text, a word added to their vocabulary backpacks to be called upon when needing to describe a wild adventure. *Rumpus*, fun to say, fairly easy to spell, conjuring a sense of wonder, might lead the parade of picture-book words that represent vocabulary development possible when picture books are read aloud or read independently.

Teaching Tips

Questions that draw attention to picture-book words:
- What do you think this word means?
- This word reminds me of…. What does it remind you of?
- Have you heard that word before? What words do we know that are like that word?
- How does the illustration help us understand the words? How do the words help us understand the illustration?
- What do you see in your mind when you hear that word (or sentence)?
- Do you think that is a real word or one made up by the author?

- Do you know this word in another language?
- Does this word name something, describe something, or explain an action (i.e., is it a noun, adjective, or verb)?
- What story comes to mind when you hear that word?
- Is this a word you might want to collect? Might you use it in your own writing?

Picture Books Aloud

"The reading of picture books can provide the occasion for performance art." (Spitz, 1998, p. 15)

Enhanced reading and listening comprehension, expanded vocabulary, motivation to engage with texts, deepened understandings about a particular topic, and recognition of ways in which language can be used in a range of contexts are among the many outcomes of read-alouds.
— Shelley Stagg Peterson (in Layne, 2015, pp. 93–94)

For more, see *Literacy Techniques* by David Booth and Larry Swartz, pp. 54-55.

Reading to children encourages literacy, promotes reading skills, and contributes to the sharing of the joy of literature. Whether children sit alongside an adult at home or gather together in the classroom and listen to a story being read aloud, they are invited to consider what the words on the page are. An adult can draw attention to these words, perhaps showing the words, pausing to discuss words, or asking questions about what may seem to be unfamiliar words. As a student hears and sees words from a favorite book, the student can begin to notice that some words occur repeatedly, leading to eventual recognition of those words. This recognition also stems from familiarity with known words in specific contexts.

Reading aloud can alter a student's attitudes to and appreciation of the developing journey toward literacy. The teacher models the joy of reading and the satisfaction that comes from making meaning with print. Teachers can use the opportunity of sharing a picture book with students of all ages to provide a meaningful opportunity for students to consider comprehension strategies. As students listen and respond to literature, they predict, make inferences, hypothesize, identify with characters, respond critically and creatively, learn information, and develop a sense of story. Along with the benefit of demonstrating and modeling how we make sense of text, the read-aloud experience is a significant opportunity to collect and celebrate and wonder about words. Vocabulary and sentence patterns are brought to life through the ear.

When reading aloud a picture book, teachers need to consider significant moments to help students contemplate an author's word choice. It is perhaps best when the paused moments are spontaneous. Stopping too many times on the read-aloud journey might be considered unfavorable, since it could take away from engagement and story appreciation. Inviting responses to words best happens when teachers reading aloud comes to pause on a word out of their own curiosity about the word or, better yet, when a student puts up a hand to share their own curiosities, wanderings, and noticings of picture book language.

Reading Aloud: A Demonstration

Excerpts are from *Teacup* by Rebecca Young and Matt Ottley

In an interactive literacy lesson, we might ask questions that help in building prior experience, inferring, predicting, visualizing, and questioning. *Teacup*, the story of a boy who is forced to journey from one home to another, is a perfect read-aloud book to help students understand bravery and hope, the refugee experience, and a search for safety. Asking questions that help students reveal and stretch their comprehension is significant. Sometimes these questions can be about the words that the author chooses:

> One there was a boy who had to leave his home and find another. In his bag he carried a book, a bottle and a blanket. In his teacup he held some earth from where he used to play.

What do you notice about the three words book, bottle, *and* blanket? *How are they similar? How are they different?*

> Some days the sea was kind, gently rocking him to sleep.

These words suggest a peace and quiet to me. What words did the author use to help the reader think about the boy's journey on the boat?

> Some days the sea was bold, and the boy tightly held to his teacup.

What pictures come to mind when you listen to that sentence? How did the words help paint a picture in your head? What might the illustration of this sentence look like?

> Some days shone bright on an endless sea of white

Did you notice that the author chose to use two rhyming words in that sentence? What other words do we know that rhyme with bright *that have the* –ight *spelling?*

Finding Word Treasures

In the Fancy Nancy picture-book series, author Jane O'Connor presents a beloved feisty character who loves fancy words:

> My favorite color is fuchsia
> That's a fancy way of saying purple.
> I like to write my name with a pen that has a plume.
> That's a fancy way of saying feather.

In a New York Times essay, O'Connor writes:

> Fancy Nancy's love of uncommon words is at the core of her uncommon nature: she dresses up everything – including what she says – to make it uniquely hers. Kids understand this. As one put it to me in a letter, "I like Fancy Nancy and the fancy words because I'm unconventional too (that's fancy for different)."

When we read (and own our own books), we might get into the habit of turning down the corners on pages, underlining a passage, putting a checkmark or asterisk in the margin, or taking a highlighter marker to the text. This reading behavior helps us to preserve words or thoughts that impress us, challenge us, or make us wonder. Most students first encounter intriguing sentences and words in picture books. In classrooms, we wouldn't encourage the turning down of pages, but the use of sticky notes can draw students' attention to an author's words. You can demonstrate this strategy by coming to a read-aloud session with two or three notes sticking to the page. As you share the book with students, explain why the notes appear by discussing the text and the words. Students can then be challenged to apply their own notes to specific pages to collect and share favorite, interesting, or new words with others in the class. Here are some examples of word-rich picture books:

Autumn arrived, with its brilliantly-colored leaves and many yellows—waxberry yellow, bumblebee yellow, mustard yellow, candle-glow yellow, maize yellow, harvest-moon yellow, even yellow ochre. But none were gold.
— from *The Gold Leaf* by Kirsten Hall; illustrated by Matthew Forsythe

Through the charred forest, over hot ash runs Dog, with a bird clamped in his big gentle mouth.
— from *Fox* by Margaret Wild; illustrated by Ron Brooks

When I was young, I lived in a city that was mean and hard and ugly. Its streets were dry as dust, cracked by heat and cold, and never blessed with rain. A gritty yellow wind blew constantly, scratching around the buildings like a hungry dog.
— from *The Promise* by Nicola Davies; illustrated by Laura Carlin

Between aspen trunks stripped cold and bare, a starving deer favors an injured leg.
— from *The Wolf-Birds* by Willow Dawson

The snow knows / where the lynx slinks / And the coyotes choir
— from *The Snow Knows* by Jennifer McGrath; illustrated by Josée Bisaillon

Sometimes I feel like a raven,
Dark and mysterious.
I am both messenger and secret keeper
And help bring light from darkness.
— from *Sometimes I Feel Like A Fox* by Danielle Daniel

Two small matching loon chicks,
in darkest downy gray,
poke and peck and pester the nest
for just one day.
— from *Loon* by Susan Vande Griek; illustrated by Karen Reczuch

Exploring Picture-Book Words

- **Visual Arts**: Students can imagine that they are the illustrator of the story. Have them choose one sentence of the picture book and create a picture that might accompany the text.
- **Glossary**: Students can create a glossary for the picture book by choosing five or six new vocabulary words. For each word, students write a definition.
- **Word Search**: Though a traditional spelling and word activity, some students may enjoy creating a word search puzzle that features 8 to 12 words from the picture book.
- **I Spy**: This works best working one-on-one or with small groups. For example, the teacher says, "I spy a word that begins with a C and ends with an N" (*crayon*); "I spy a word that has the word art hidden inside it" (*heart*).
- **Pattern Focus**: Students can work alone or with a partner to inspect and collect words that fit a specific pattern; e.g., find plural words; find adjectives; find three-syllable words; find words with double vowels; find words that end with three consonants. It is best to assign only one focus spelling pattern for this activity. For young readers, the challenge can be simplified by suggesting they discover three to five words. Some students

may be able to collect more than five words for an assigned spelling pattern.

Appreciating Novel Words

A close study of the language and structure of a novel can help students discover the elements of distinctive, successful writing. When students focus on style—the way the novelist uses words, sentences, and paragraphs to paint images, arouse emotions, and build narrative—you can help them to isolate these elements. To learn about the language of literature, students should be encouraged to look closely at the word choice used by an author and discuss the deliberate choices an author makes to convey his or her message. Students have opportunities to enrich their literary knowledge when they reflect and respond to the way the authors write: how they describe characters and setting, how they use dialogue, how they arrange words, how they use familiar words and introduce new ones. The strategies and activities presented here have students inspect words in novels and consider how they help them respond to the plot, character, setting, and theme of the novel.

Bookshelf: Remarkable Novels

An asterisk (*) marks books for young adults.

Katherine Applegate. *Wishtree* (also *Endling #1: The Last*)
Dusti Bowling. *Insignificant Events in the Life of a Cactus*
Kate DiCamillo. *Louisiana's Way Home*
Shari Green. *Missing Mike*
Alan Gratz. *Refugee*
Veera Hiranandani. *The Night Diary*
Erin Entrada Kelly. *You Go First*
Wendy Mass & Rebecca Stead. *Bob*
David Barclay Moore. *The Stars Beneath Our Feet*
Jason Reynolds. *Ghost*; *Patina*; *Sunny*; *Lu* (Track series)
Jewell Parker Rhodes. *Ghost Boys*
Heather Smith. *Ebb & Flow* (also *The Agony of Bun O'Keefe**)
Eric Walters. *90 Days of Different**
Kelly Yang. *Front Desk*

Finding and presenting meaningful passages from fiction that show characters who are curious about words can serve as significant models for students to consider their own finesse with words and to explore and cherish words. The novel excerpts under the head Novels with Characters Who Are Word Collectors on page 74 serve as examples that can be shared with students. One or more of these passages can be presented as a shared reading activity, guided by the following questions:

- How do we know these novel characters enjoy word collecting?
- Which words collected by the characters are familiar to you? Have you used these words in your own writing?
- What connections do you make to this excerpted text?
- As you read this passage, what do you wonder about?
- Does this excerpt encourage you to read the novel independently? Explain.

Novels with Characters Who Are Word Collectors

Booked by Kwame Alexander

In the free-verse novel *Booked*, protagonist Nick Hall, soccer hero, is often up against his father, a linguistic professor with chronic *verbomania* as evidenced by the fact that he actually wrote a dictionary called *Weird and Wonderful Words*— with footnotes. Alexander inserts unusual and wonderful words throughout the novel with accompanying footnotes.

> *The good colleges look for extraordinary, Nicholas. You*
> *Need to know these words if you want to attend a good*
> *College, Nicholas.*
> College is not for, like, five years, Dad.
> *Placement tests. Application essays. It's all words, son.*
> *Know the words and you'll excel.*
> None of my friends have to memorize a thousand words. I'm not like you, Dad.
> Maybe I don't want to be extraordinary. Maybe I just want to be ordinary.
> *That's a load of codswallop. I give you the dictionary so you'll know the world better,*
> *son. So you'll BE better.*

Missing Mike by Shari Green

Cara Donovan and her family are victims of a wildfire disaster. Forced to evacuate, forced to abandon her beloved one-eyed dog Mike, Cara finds some comfort with a favorite pastime—completing crossword puzzles. Spread throughout the free-verse novel are words for her to solve; e.g., "absence of hope" (7 letters): *despair*. Seeking a word that best matches one for "home," Cara thinks:

> I bet if you asked one hundred people
> you'd probably find
> there are one hundred words
> for home.

Word Nerd by Susin Nielsen

Twelve-year old Ambrose lives in basement apartment with his mother. Ambrose is seeking a place of belonging and acceptance. When he strikes up a friendship with the landlord's son Cosmos, he discovers that they each share a love of the game Scrabble. The lead of each chapter in the novel features seven scrabble titles and a list of Scrabble words that can be formed from the titles. The chapter title subsequently becomes an anagram using all seven letters. Here is an example from Chapter One:

> LGRYALE
> Early, ale, all, gall, gel, leg, real, gear, largely, lag, gale
> Chapter title: ALLERGY

You Go First by Erin Entrada Kelly

Charlotte Lockard and Ben Boxer live in different states but become connected by a love of online Scrabble. Their worlds are connected beyond words, as each character struggles to find a place of belonging both in and out of school. This fine novel, told in alternating voices, helps readers to learn the meaning of such words as Xylitol (a cavity-fighting additive), and to understand the meaning of resilience. Charlotte is a lover of words and a hoarder of scientific, artistic, and human facts. When she realizes some girls make fun of her of because her rock collection, she wonders:

> Did they know what a turquenite was? Could they pick an aventurine out of a line? Could they define ingeneous differentiation and fractional crystallization?

Ebb & Flow by Heather Smith

In the novel *Ebb & Flow*, Jett and his Grandma enjoy puns as well as playing games of Scrabble:

> When Grandma laid words
> Like JACAMA
> and MUNDANE
> I bit my lip
> And wrinkled my nose.

Exploring Novel Words

100-Word Book Blurb

100 words provides an opportunity for students to create a synopsis or book blurb that tells others about a novel that has been read. One purpose of the book synopsis is to interest others in the book, to persuade them to read it. So there needs to be a balance between highlighting the plot and problems of the novel and not giving too much away. When preparing a novel synopsis, the writer needs to

- Summarize the plot
- Describe the major conflict
- Introduce the characters and describe their relationships to one another
- Highlight the main theme(s) of the novel

Extension: As a class, students can post synopses on a class website to inform and invite others to read the recommended books.

Direct students to prepare a synopsis of the novel by writing a summary of exactly 100 words. Doing so will require students to continue to revise and edit, endeavoring to choose the best words possible to inform others about the book. Once their book blurbs are completed, students find a partner who has written a synopsis for the same novel. Partners compare ideas and then combine them to make a new summary that is exactly 100 words long.

36-Word Book Report

This activity encourages students to choose words carefully to summarize a novel. Present 36-Word Book Report template on page 86 to students and have them complete the word pyramid:

> 1 word that explains the theme of the novel
> 2 words that express your opinion of the novel
> 3 words that describe the setting
> 4 words that describe the main character
> 5 characters' names
> 6 new words you discovered in the novel
> 7 words that summarize the main problem at the heart of the novel
> 8 words that summarize the plot

Once their report is completed, students can work with a partner who completed a pyramid on the same title and compare their word choices.

Here is a sample 36-Word Book
Report on *Sweep: The Story of a
Girl and Her Monster* by Jonathan
Auxier.

perseverance
strong   writing
Victorian   England   chimneys
loving   resilient   hopeful   wise
Nan   Charlie   Crudd   Miss Bloom   Toby
golem   char   offal   flues   dander   bespoke
Child   chimney   sweeps   struggle   to   survive   abuse
Young   girl   and   protective   soot   monster   bond   together

Extension

Students meet in groups of four or five, each student having read a different novel. Students use their novel pyramids to report their summary of the book, highlighting the characters, plot, setting, conflict, and themes of the story.

Going on a Word Hunt

This activity helps students to investigate the words, sentences, and dialogue an author used in a novel. For each item listed (see also the Word Hunt template on page 87), students record a word, sentence, or phrase from any novel they have read:

1. Write the first sentence of the novel.
2. Write the last sentence of the novel.
3. What is the longest word in the title of the novel?
4. Turn to page 45 and 46. Find and record a line of dialogue, if possible.
5. Turn to pages 66 and 67. Find and record three adjectives that the author used.
6. Find and record the first three words that appear on the top of pages 98, 99, and 100. Circle any words with three syllables.
7. Turn to the second-last page. Write three of the longest words you can find on that page.
8. Find and record the first sentence of the second paragraph on the third page.
9. Find and record any sentence that is exactly 12 words long.
10. Record two or three words from the novel that you never knew before.
11. Write the author's full name. How many different consonants appear in the name?
12. Find and record one or more sentences that paint a strong picture in your mind.

Once they are done, students can compare answers with someone who has worked with the same novel.

Using Sentence Snippets

This strategy encourages students to collect sentences from novels they particularly admire because of the way the author has chosen and arranged the words. These sentences paint a vivid picture of a character or setting, or effectively summarized the plot of the story:

> I've never been in an earthquake. Don't know if this was even close to how they are, but the ground definitely felt like it opened up and ate me.
> — from *Long Way Down* by Jason Reynolds

And as I sat beneath fluorescent cylinders spewing aggressively artificial light, I thought about how we all believed ourselves to be the hero of some personal epic, when in fact we were basically identical organisms colonizing a vast and windowless room that smelled of Lysol and lard.
— from *Turtles All the Way Down* by John Green

Steam rose from the soil like a phantom, carrying with it a whisper of autumn smoke that had been lying dormant in the frosty ground.
— from *The Night Gardener* by Jonathan Auxier

It was the autumn of 1943 when my steady life began to spin, not only because of the war that had drawn the whole world into a screaming brawl, but also because of the darkhearted girl who came to our hills and changed everything.
— from *Wolf Hollow* by Lauren Wolk

In the Classroom: When Words Paint Pictures
by Elaine Eisen, Grade 4 Teacher

As my students closed their eyes, I read aloud the following sentences from the first pages of novel *Sweep* by Jonathan Auxier:

> There are all sorts of wonderful things a person might see very early in the morning. You might see your parents sleeping. You might see an ambitious bird catching a worm. You might see an unclaimed penny on the sidewalk or the first rays of dawn. And if you are very, very lucky, you might even catch a glimpse of the girl and her Sweep.

Students were then instructed to open their eyes, turn, and talk to share what they saw inside their minds as they listened to the text fragment. They discussed different colors of an early morning, a close up look at a penny, a girl following behind a man carrying a large broom. One girl declared, "We all had different pictures in our heads!" Clearly, my students understood that the visual picture each of us builds from reading or listening to a text differs from that of the person sitting alongside us.

How can I help students slow down, pause, and scrutinize the way a novelist put words together to paint a picture in the reader's head? What is a meaningful way to teach the comprehension strategy of Visualization? If my goal is to have students pay careful attention to the vocabulary they encounter in their reading and better consider an author's style and use of language, I knew that it was important to provide activities that would demonstrate and make explicit a writer's wordcrafting.

Just as an artist chooses from a colorful palette to create a painting or a chef considers the ingredients and the amount of the ingredients to create a tasty dish, writers use words to put thoughts onto paper. Of course, the written word serves many functions, but when an author's words help readers of fiction to visualize what is happening in the text they are helping them to imagine what they are reading. Words capture ideas and feelings and often help to make movies in our heads.

Phase One: Isolating novel snippets

The students in my class are eager readers of novels. For independent reading time, I provided students with sticky notes to put on pages in which they met "great" sentences that prompted visualization. Students were then given a file card to copy one favorite sentence that struck their imaginations. In small groups, students shared their novel snippets by discussing the author's word choices and how effective those words are at creating an image of a character, setting, or story event.

Phase Two: Creating illustrations from novel snippets

The next phase of the lesson invited students to create illustrations to bring those words alive. Students were familiar with the concept of both the words and visual images of a picture book engaging the reader, but most of the novels that my students were reading were not illustrated. If the novel did include illustrations, what might they expect the pictures to be? How might the illustration connect to or extend the verbal text? I limited the students to the use of black markers to create drawings using their novel snippets as sources. The activity went a bit beyond "draw a picture of your favorite scene." The snippets activity encouraged students to draw images suggested by text with a focus on novel words, thereby bringing meaning to the words and illuminating the words through art.

Sometimes when I read books that I own, I turn down the corner of a page that intrigues me. I can also take a highlighter marker or underline passages that I connect to or that make me wonder. Sometimes I added a sticky note to certain pages. The novel snippet activity helped students to highlight, underline, and pay attention to words. Isolating a fragment of a text can help students understand an author chooses words carefully to engage, inform, and appeal to the reader's thoughts, senses, and imagination. Paying attention to a novel snippet can lead students to consider other powerful sentences they encounter in their reading and can, we hope, influence their choice of words in their own writing. Words and sentences that make you make go, "Ahhh!"

Snippet from *The Frame Up* by Wendy McLeod MacKnight

Drawing by Grace L. Snippet from *Boy* by Roald Dahl

78

Phase Three: Creating Free-Verse Poems

To extend the learning and have students pay further closer attention to the words of the novel, I provided students with instructions about transforming a novel snippet into a free-verse poem.

1. I began by displaying the following sentence from the novel *Pax* by Sara Pennypacker on the interactive whiteboard:

> The sharp odors of pine—wood, bark, cones, and needles—slivered through the air like blades, but beneath that the fox recognized softer clover and wild garlic and ferns, and also a hundred things he had never encountered before but that smelled green and urgent.
> — from *Pax* by Sara Pennypacker

2. As a class, we discussed possible line breaks where sentence could be divided to emphasize thoughts and images into sections one, two, three, or possibly four words in length.

> The sharp odors of pine / —wood, bark, cones, and needles— / slivered through the air / like blades, / but beneath that the fox recognized softer clover / and wild garlic / and ferns, / and also a hundred things / he had never encountered before / but that smelled green / and urgent.

3. A demonstration showed how this sentence could be transformed into a free-verse poem by adding white spaces to represent indentations or breaks between stanzas:

> The sharp odors of pine
>   —wood, bark, cones, and needles—
> slivered through the air
> like blades,
>   but beneath that the fox recognized
>   softer clover
>   and wild garlic
>   and ferns,
> and also a hundred things he had never encountered before
>   but that smelled green
>   and urgent.

4. Students then explored the process by choosing snippets or fragments from the novels they were reading. Here are two examples:

> The great dark trees
> of the big woods
>   stood all around the house
>   And beyond them
>   Were other trees
>   and beyond them
>   Were more trees
> — from the novel *Little House in the Big Woods* by Laura Ingalls Wilder

Her head turned
As she noticed
The ink drawing
Now looking for all the world
Like a rough-sketched blackbird
In three dimensions
Fly up the
Mizzen mast.
— from the novel *The Map to Everywhere* by Carrie Ryan and John Parke Davis

Teaching Tips

- It is best to demonstrate the process with students, inviting individuals to make suggestions for line breaks.
- Using an interactive whiteboard provides an opportunity for students to witness how words and line lengths can be continually manipulated.
- Each student (or student pair) in the class can be given the same excerpted sentence to work on. Once poems are completed, students can compare poems to note similarities and differences.
- This activity is best done on a computer, where students can easily manipulate text until they are satisfied with a free-verse format. Students may choose to change the font for some words to create a visual impact for the poem.

Using Graphic Organizers

Graphic organizers can be used to help students inspect, respect, and collect words.

Look at the Word I Found

The Look at the Word I Found graphic organizer on page 88 can be used to help students record words that interest them while they read fiction. The activity of recording words they've discovered helps draw students' attention to collecting vocabulary that they can both share with others and choose to use in their own future writing. The chart invites students to record the date, the interesting word, the piece of text where the word is located, and the sentence in which the word appears (page number is optional).

Look at the Word I Found Sample

Date	Word I Found	What I Read	Sentence
12/11	perilous	*Ghost Boys* by Jewell Parker Rhodes	In this neighborhood, getting a child to adulthood is perilous. (page 13)

My Collect-a-Word Calendar

A calendar can be used for students to record words that they collected from their reading, listening, and viewing. This can be done over a month-long period or over the school year—180 school days means 180 words collected over one year!

Word Web

See page 90 for the Word Web template. In the centre circle, students record the word they've collected. Students complete each of the web circles to provide more information about the word:

> Centre circle: Word
> Upper left circle: A picture
> Upper right circle: Online definition
> Bottom left circle: The word used in a sentence
> Bottom right circle: What you might know about where the word comes from

Invented Worlds, Invented Words

Katherine Applegate is a great author. I am very fond of her novels for young people and regard *Home of the Brave*, *Crenshaw*, and *Wishtree* among my favorite reads over the past decade. She is the author of the popular Animorphs series and has won the Newbery Medal for the novel *The One and Only Ivan*. I look forward to reading any new Applegate titles. In 2018, Applegate gave the world a remarkable fantasy adventure title, *Endling #1: The Last*, the first in a series. I am not a fan of science fiction or fantasy fiction, so I delved into the book with some trepidation but also eagerness, knowing that Applegate is a master storyteller and has a command of stories with anthropomorphic characters.

Byx appears to be a dog but is able to walk upright, has a luxurious coat of fur, and has the ability to determine whether someone is telling the truth or not. Byx is the youngest of her dairne pack, and fears she might be the Endling, the last one left. Dairne? Byx? Endling? With these words I knew I was entering a newly invented world, with newly invented character names, strange place names, and invented narratives around good and evil happenings.

Who's to say whether the vocabulary presented in this book will become popularized or familiarized, but I have a hunch that *Endling #1: The Last* can easily sit alongside books by renowned children's authors Dr. Seuss, Roald Dahl, J.K. Rowling, and Lewis Carroll. These writers reign in the world of made-up words which have delighted and engaged millions and millions of young readers (and older ones too).

Inventive Authors

Dr. Seuss

The first documented appearance of the word *nerd* is in the Dr. Seuss's book *If I Ran the Zoo* (1950). The first published use of the word is in an article written in 1951 for *Newsweek* magazine: "In Detroit, someone who was once called a drip or a square is now regrettably a nerd." In 1960, Bennett Cerf, the co-founder of Random House publishing, challenged Dr. Seuss to write a book containing only 50 different words that would entertain young children. Dr. Seuss took the bet;

he selected words from a first-grade vocabulary list and produced *Green Eggs and Ham.*

Here are ten six-letter words invented by Dr. Seuss:

gootch	skritz
Grinch	thneed
kweet	wocket
lerkim	zillow
nizzard	zummer

Roald Dahl

Roald Dahl provided a new "lexicon of the imagination" encouraging young readers to stretch and experiment with language in such books as *The BFG, The Witches,* and especially *Charlie and the Chocolate Factory.*

Here are nine words invented by Roald Dahl. Which are tasty treats? Which are creatures?

Fizzwinkles	Plushnuggets
Frothblowers	Snozzwanger
Hornswogglers	Sptisizzfers
Oompa Loompas	Whangdoodle
Phizzwizard	

J.K. Rowling

When it comes to new language for a new century, J.K. Rowling reigns supreme. The universe of Harry Potter has given readers a whole new vocabulary particular to the story world created by the author, and has put invented terminology into mainstream use—and into modern dictionaries. Some of the words may pre-exist Rowling's work, but what is particularly noteworthy is the way the author has used and combined real words into new inventive concepts.

Here are some magical items that appear in the Harry Potter Books

Bezoar: stone taken from an animal's stomach

Diffindo: a charm

Engorgio: an engorgement charm

Foe-glass: magic mirror in which you can see enemies

Gillyweed: a water plant; if you eat it, you temporarily grow fins

Howler: a wizard letter that comes in a red envelope and shouts the message

Knut: bronze wizard money

Niffler: a creature that can find buried treasure

Pensieve: a magical instrument used to view memories

Relashio: spell to make someone release their hold

For a complete glossary of words invented by J.K. Rowling, see http://harrypotter.scholastic.com/

Lewis Carroll

The poem "Jabberwocky" serves as a classic example of invented language from the world of children's literature. Since the character of Alice is new to the invented world through the looking glass, her education becomes ours.

"You seem very clever at explaining words, Sir," said Alice. "Would you kindly tell me the meaning of the poem called 'Jabberwocky'?"

Alice repeated the first verse:

'Twas brillig, and the slithy toves

Did gyre and gimble in the wabe:

All mimsy were the borogroves,
and the mome raths outgrabe

"That's enough to begin with," Humpty Dumpty interrupted. "There are plenty of hard words there. 'Brillig' means four o'clock in the afternoon—the time you begin broiling things for dinner."

"That'll do very well," said Alice. "And 'slithy'?"

"Well, 'slithy' just means 'lithe and slimy'. 'Lithe' is the same as 'active'. See, it's like a portmanteau—there are two meanings packed up into one word."

— from *Through the Looking Glass* by Lewis Carroll

Ten Popular Fantasy Authors

Eoin Colfer	Garth Nix
Diane Duane	Philip Pullman
Cornelia Funke	Ransom Riggs
Erin Hunter	J.K. Rowling
Ursula K. Le Guin	J.R.R. Tokien

Collecting Invented Words

Encourage students to collect words that have been invented or redefined by authors of science fiction, speculative fiction, and fantasy. Students can

- Create a glossary of terms to assist readers of the book(s)
- Use one or more invented words in their own narrative writing
- Create an illustration for the novel that would give additional information on the unique people, places, or things that have been invented by the author

Becoming a Word Inventor

These word beginnings and endings are drawn from languages invented by Dr. Seuss, Roald Dahl, J.K. Rowling, and Lewis Carroll.

Students can invent a new vocabulary of eight to ten words. Have students match items from Column 1 with an item from Column 2 to invent a new word. Items can be used more than once, if necessary.

Column 1		Column 2	
Snozz	Ani	winkle	nuggets
Whang	Pens	woggler	magus
Jabber	Verm	esco	ditch
Evan	Brill	wocky	ate
Azka	Thneed	wart	bleck
Quid	Mim	ig	icious
Fizz	Hinky	loompa	sy
Plush		ala	

Extensions

- Once students have compiled a list of eight to ten new words, have them provide a brief definition of the word and/or create an illustration that would help explain the word.
- As a further extension, some students may wish to write a narrative that includes one or more of their newly invented words as the names of characters, settings, or objects.

Special Words for Special Subjects

Any discussion of the words that filter through our classrooms must include recognition of vocabulary that appears in the content areas. Each grade level presents specialized vocabulary for mathematics, science and technology, social studies (geography and history), physical and health education, and the arts (dance, drama, music, visual arts). Much of the nonfiction text that students encounter when investigating topics in curriculum areas introduces them to words that might not be familiar to them but are relevant for gaining information about a topic:

- Math words, such as *algorithm*, *isosceles*, *numerator*, *perpendicular*, *probability*, *polygon*, *radius*, and *rhombus*, help students interpret and apply concepts in number sense, geometry, or data management.
- Extended experiences with such words as *buoyancy*, *compression*, *invertebrate*, *kinetic*, *omnivore*, *sedimentary*, *species*, and *tension* can help to build a background in science.
- Knowledge in social studies grows by learning such new words as *artifact*, *colony*, *community*, *democracy*, *identity*, *economy*, *government*, *landform*, *longitude*, *resources*, *settlement*, and *trade*.
- Having arts terminology, such as *beat*, *caricature*, *choreography*, *collage*, *etching*, *gamelan*, *gesture*, *perspective*, *prop*, *rhythm*, *tempo*, and *texture*, helps students engage in the creative process as they explore, share, and present their work.

Most often, content vocabulary needs to be explicitly taught so that students have an understanding of the information presented to them in the subject. The words may be unfamiliar or disconnected to students, so it is important that we explain what these words mean, with examples, in order to help our students at any grade level be comfortable when exploring topics we introduce into the program. Most curriculum documents outline expectations that students will be able to accurately use domain-specific words and phrases that are grade-appropriate. By using subject-specific words, students can make better connections to the concepts explored in the curriculum area. Moreover, their background knowledge in these subjects is enriched, preparing them to understand and use these words as their educational journey and life experiences continue.

Teaching Tips

- Content vocabulary should be available on a word wall or chart of specialized vocabulary for students to refer to when exploring a strand in the curriculum. Students will most likely use this as a spelling reference when required to use the words in their writing.

- It is common in summative or standardized tests that students are asked questions that assess their understanding of vocabulary. To prepare students for quizzes or tests, it is important to review a glossary of terms for topics explored in class. Students don't have to memorize definitions of the words, but should feel comfortable knowing what words mean and be able to provide a context where these words might be used.
- When conducting research or preparing a report, students should be encouraged to highlight unfamiliar vocabulary and present information by using a diagram or illustration, a definition or glossary that helps explain the word.

Sorting Curriculum Words

Have students work alone or with a partner to sort vocabulary words. Students can prepare a list of words that they think are appropriate for each curriculum topic. Some words may be placed in more than one box. This activity can be adapted by presenting words specific to a grade.

adaptation	equation	operation
composition	estimation	percussion
compression	exploration	precipitation
condensation	expression	population
creation	fraction	rotation
decomposition	gradation	solution
dimension	improvisation	tension
division	migration	tessellation
elevation	musician	
emigration	notation	

Extension: Have students put an asterisk (*) beside one word in each box that they would like to learn more about. Students can use the Internet to find the meanings and sample sentences of four words that they've marked.

Social Studies (Geography, History) *immigration* *population*	Science and Technology *condensation*
Mathematics *fraction*	The Arts (Dance, Drama, Music, Visual Arts) *notation*

36-Word Book Report

Name: _____   Novel Title: _____

_____

_____ _____

_____ _____ _____

_____ _____ _____ _____

_____ _____ _____ _____ _____

_____ _____ _____ _____ _____ _____

_____ _____ _____ _____ _____ _____ _____

_____ _____ _____ _____ _____ _____ _____ _____

1 word that explains the theme of the novel

2 words that express your opinion of the novel

3 words that describe the setting

4 words that describe the main character

5 characters' names

6 new words you discovered in the novel

7 words that summarize the main problem at the heart of the novel

8 words that summarize the plot

Share your report with one or two people who have not read this book. Be prepared to discuss the novel by explaining your word choices.

Pembroke Publishers ©2019 *Word by Word* by Larry Swartz ISBN 978-1-55138-338-5

Word Hunt

Name: _____   Book Title: _____

1. Write the first sentence of the novel.

2. Write the last sentence of the novel.

3. What is the longest word in the title of the novel?

4. Turn to page 45 and 46. Find and record a line of dialogue, if possible.

5. Turn to pages 66 and 67. Find and record three adjectives that the author used.

   _____   _____   _____

6. Find and record the first three words that appear on the top of pages 98, 99, and 100. Circle any words with three syllables.

   _____   _____   _____

7. Turn to the second-last page. Write three of the longest words you can find on that page.

   _____   _____   _____

8. Find and record the first sentence of the second paragraph on the third page.

9. Find and record any sentence that is exactly 12 words long.

10. Record two or three words from the novel that you never knew before.

11. Write the author's full name. How many different consonants appear in the name?

12. Find and record one or more sentences that paint a strong picture in your mind.

Pembroke Publishers ©2019 *Word by Word* by Larry Swartz ISBN 978-1-55138-338-5

Look at the Word I Found

Name: _____

Date	Word	What I Read	Sentence

Pembroke Publishers ©2019 *Word by Word* by Larry Swartz ISBN 978-1-55138-338-5

My Collect-a-Word Calendar

Name: _____

Month: _____

Sunday	Monday	Tuesday	Wednesday	Thursday	Friday	Saturday

Pembroke Publishers ©2019 *Word by Word* by Larry Swartz ISBN 978-1-55138-338-5

Word Web

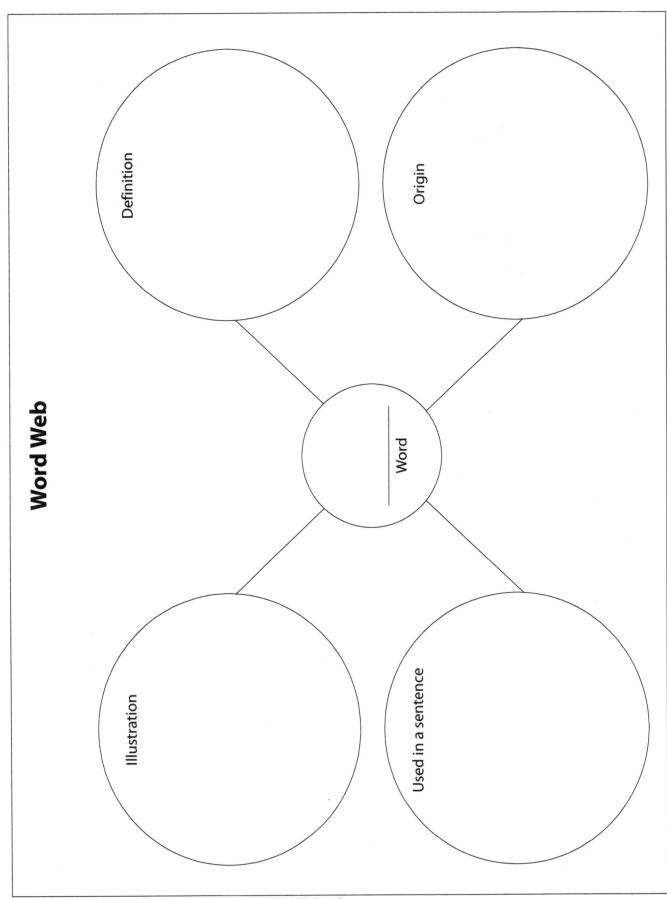

Definition

Origin

Word
_____

Illustration

Used in a sentence

Pembroke Publishers ©2019 *Word by Word* by Larry Swartz ISBN 978-1-55138-338-5

6

The Poetry of Words

There is no Frigate like a Book
To take us to Lands away
Nor any Coursers like a Page
Of prancing Poetry—
— Emily Dickinson

In the introduction to her new poetry anthology *Voices in the Air: Poems for Listeners*, Naomi Shihab Nye writes about an important word:

> Recently, when I had the honor of visiting Yokohama International School in Japan to conduct poetry workshops, student Juna Hewitt taught me an important word—Yutori—"life-space". She listed various interpretations for its meaning— arriving early, so you don't have to rush. Giving yourself room to make a mistake... Juna said she felt that reading and writing poetry gives us more yutori—a place to stand back to contemplate what we are living and experiencing. More spaciousness in being, more room in which to listen. I love this. It was the best word I learned all year. (Nye, 2018)

When I was in school, no one told me that poetry could be fun, that I could play with poems, and that I could delight in poem words in so many ways. I always felt that I had to unlock the mystery (that the teacher knew the answer to) of a poem's meaning, and I rather disliked having to memorize poems, which was one of the main events I remember from middle and high school. In the past decades, we have made great strides in the area of children's poetry, seeing the value of poetry as an art experience. Using poetry in the classroom can enhance learning, not only for reading and writing, but also for discussing, questioning, performing, painting, singing, and dancing. It is an art form that allows us to pay attention to words—and the music behind the words.

In the introduction to *The Poetry Experience*, poet Sheree Fitch writes:

> Those who teach poetry with passion and joy know it is one of the richest learning experiences students can have. We journey to worlds and peer into spaces in our hearts and minds and souls through poetry. Poetry is word music, an art form that belongs to a rich oral tradition that pre-dates the written word. At its most serious, poetry rattles us to the core of our being. Verse of the most nonsensical kind urges us, like an itch, to scratch and burst forth into a silly slide of syllables ourselves. … A poem can be read in solitude and silence, of course, and a connection is made between the poet and the reader. But the inner ear will still hear the chime in the rhyme, the beat in the feet, the inherent musicality of every word. When poetry is lifted off the page and shared, it connects us to each other. (Fitch & Swartz, 2008, p. 4)

In his book, *Words That Taste Good*, word scavenger Bill Moore explores more than 600 short, sharp bits of poetry to stimulate interest in the power of words. Moore explains:

> Poets work with words and words are peculiar things. They are very hard to pin down. They slither away from you and yet they are the very best way of conveying ideas, thoughts and emotions. (Moore, 1987, p. 2)

When we incorporate poetry into the literacy lives of students, we are providing opportunities to not only demonstrate the power of language, but also open up responses that are personal, reflective, and often emotional. When writing poems, students are challenged to carefully consider word choices to express ideas and feelings. Offering poems that students are excited about reading, listening to, reading chorally, and responding to through talk, writing, or artistic mediums can lead students to discover favorite poems, cherish words by heart, and come to a better understanding of how reading poems aloud encourages readers to manipulate the sounds of words, and how creating poems invites writers to become wordsmiths. In this chapter, students will have opportunities to

- Collect interesting, amusing, fascinating, puzzling words from poems
- Follow a poem pattern and carefully make word choices to create an image, thought, and/or feeling
- Compose poems by following a formula that creates a particular poetic form (e.g. rhyming couplet, haiku)
- Appreciate how a poet's words can effectively create pictures in the mind and appeal to the senses by examining snippets/fragments of poems
- Practice the blackout poetry technique to isolate and highlight words from a text
- Participate in large and small groups to read poems aloud chorally
- Build word knowledge by responding to short poems in writing

Poets as Wordsmiths

- The very first skill the poet must employ, before all others, is the choice of the right words.
- No two persons have the same response to any word.
- Poets paint pictures with words, as painters do with color and shape.
- Poets are wordsmiths. They spend their lives choosing words, bending them, shaping them, teasing them, playing with them. The sounds of language fascinate them so.

- Poets shape their poems by the way they arrange words on the paper.
- Poets make good reporters: they see and hear with special eyes and ears.
- Something in the poet's words may trigger vivid recollections from our past.
- Words are the tools with which the poem is built, and we must be aware of their power.
- The poet writes and wants to manipulate the reader's mind. The emotional connotation of words is one of the chief weapons.
- Poets feel something powerfully; they put their feelings into words and hope that we, hearing those words, will hear an echo of their original feelings.
- Words say something of the inaudible music that moves along in our bodies from moment to moment like water in a river.

(Booth & Moore, 2003)

Bookshelf: Poetry Anthologies by David Booth

Bird Guy; illus. Maya Ishiura
The Bully, The Bullied, The Bystander, The Brave (edited with Larry Swartz)
Dr. Knickerbocker and Other Rhymes (editor); illus. Maryann Kovalski
Head to Toe Spaghetti and Other Tasty Poems; illus. Les Drew
Images of Nature (editor); art by The Group of Seven
'Til All the Stars Have Fallen (editor); illus. Kady MacDonald Denton

Collecting Poem Words

We can collect, inspect, and respect poem words for many different reasons. To explore how the language of poetry can be considered special, it is important to highlight these words and consider their importance by considering different categories, such as the ones listed below.

Rhyme Words

Some prefer cooking
In great iron pots.
Others like dicing
And slicing shallots.
— David Booth, from "Our Stomachs Are Shouting" in *Head to Toe Spaghetti*

Invented Words

Spring is showery,
  flowery, bowery
Summer is hoppy
  croppy, poppy;
Autumn is wheezy
  sneezy, freezy
Winter is slippy,
  drippy, nippy.
— Mother Goose

Word Pictures

Lean a ladder
Against the moon
And climb, climb high
Talk to the stars
And leave your handprints
All across the sky
— Sheree Fitch, from "Ladder to the Sky" in *Toes in My Nose*

Word Sounds

As I sat in the gloaming
I heard a voice say,
"Weep no more, sigh no more;
Come, come away!"
— Walter de la Mare, from "The Voice"

I love the crunch of potato chips
I love the munch of potato chips
   Cruncha Cruncha
   Muncha Muncha
Potato chips for snack
Or Luncha!
— Larry Swartz, "Potato Chips"

Exploring Poem Words

Poem of the Day

A poem-a-day can be an important ritual in the classroom, inviting exposure to a variety of forms, a range of poets, a banquet of words.

On most days, the activity can last for just a few moments; on other days, students can linger over a poem, perhaps through shared reading, drama, written and/or oral response, or arts activities. A poem can be chosen from a single poet, or according to a theme or poetic form. Students can consider the form, theme, and impact of the poem. But in order to draw attention to word choices, we help students

- notice rhyming words
- discuss unfamiliar words
- highlight similes, metaphors
- consider alliteration
- respond to the choice of adjectives, verbs, and adverbs that add to the appeal of the poem

Teaching Tip

Once you have modeled how to present a poem each day, students can be assigned the responsibility of introducing poems to the class. A student can be assigned to be the poet wizard for a day (a week?) and choose a favorite poem from an anthology that appeals to them. Poet wizards can read the poem from an anthology, but transcribing poems on a chart or displaying the poem on the interactive whiteboard helps everyone examine the poem's forms and carefully consider the poem's vocabulary.

Exploring the Free-Verse Novel

Many recent free-verse novels present the refugee experience; in studying these stories, students can learn about the past, present, and future lives of characters caught in the web of finding a new place of belonging: *Home of the Brave* by Katherine Applegate; *All the Broken Pieces* by Ann E. Burg; *Inside Out and Back Again* by Thanhha Lai.

Gaining popularity over the past two decades has been the free-verse novel, usually a series of free-verse poems presented in a sequence that builds a narrative. Each poem is usually no more than two or three pages in length. This innovative novel form can be introduced into your language arts program, where students in groups can dig deeper into a title.

Ebb & Flow by Canadian author Heather Smith is a sublime example of free-verse narrative. After experiencing a unsettling incident in a new town, Jett returns to the coast of Newfoundland to spend the summer with his grandmother, hoping to forget and to get revived. Presenting a single poem from the collection can help students understand how authors carefully choose and manipulate words to create images in the head, evoke emotions, and build narrative.

> **Pounding**
> As we pulled up
> to the little wooden house
> on the rocky eastern shore
> my heart went
> crazy,
> pounding,
> like the crashing waves
> I could hear in the distance,
> I was so happy to be back,
> I almost forgot
> I was there to forget.

The appeal of free-verse novels for word exploration may be attributed to the following:

- Words take a very visual aspect, depending on how the author constructs the verse.
- Lines are usually short, sometimes with one or two words, sometimes five or six words, which may not be as intimidating to some readers as full lines of prose text.
- Each poem seems to end with a punch, something to linger over.
- Strong images are conveyed in brevity, appealing to the senses.
- Poems serve as a model for students creating their own free-verse poems.

Bookshelf: Free-Verse Novels for Readers of Different Ages

Ages 7–9: *Little Dog Lost* by Marion Dane Bauer; *Love That Dog* by Sharon Creech; *Gone Fishing* by Tamera Will Wissinger

Ages 9–12: *Home of the Brave* by Katherine Applegate; *Unbound* by Ann E. Burg; *Missing Mike* by Shari Green; *The Red Pencil* by Andrea Davis Pinkney

Ages 12 +: *Solo* by Kwame Alexander; *Long Way Down* by Jason Reynolds; *Brown Girl Dreaming* by Jacqueline Woodson

Bookshelf: Award-Winning Free-Verse Novels

Kwame Alexander. *The Crossover* (2015 Newbery Medal) (also *Booked, Rebound*)

Karen Hesse. *Out of the Dust* (1998 Newbery Medal)

Thanhha Lai. *Inside Out and Back Again* (2011 National Book Award Winner)

Caroline Pignat. *The Gospel Truth* (2015 Governor General's Award Winner)

Pamela Porter. *The Crazy Man* (2005 Governor General's Award; TD Canadian Children's Literature Award)

Creating Blackout Poetry

re·dact
ra'dakt/
verb
past tense: redacted; past participle: redacted
1. edit (text) for publication.
• censor or obscure (part of a text) for legal or security purposes

A blackout poem is created when a poet takes a marker (usually black) to an already established text and starts redacting words until a poem is formed. The key thing with a blackout poem is that, together, the text and redacted text form a sort of visual poem. Blackout poets are encouraged to cross out the majority of the existing found text, leaving visible only words that comprise a new poem. Blackout poets create a new piece of art from an existing piece of art.

This activity is ideally done with a short newspaper or magazine article. However, photocopied excerpts from fiction or nonfiction texts can also be used to create blackout poetry. A fun way to experience blackout poetry is to use books that are being discarded. Students can each take a page from the book and use it to create a blackout poem.

After reading a text, students can use one of the following processes:

- Use a black marker liberally to black out words they consider to be not particularly essential for understanding the text. The words that remain on the page remain make up a free-verse poem.
- Use the computer to black out words.

Teaching Tips

- Students are encouraged to finalize the activity with a minimum number of words. Once they have initially gone through the blackout process, they can review once again and continue to eliminate words.
- No matter how the blackout process is done, students can use the computer to re-write and format the remaining words as a free-verse poem

---

In the Classroom: Blackout Poetry
by Ernest Agbuya, Grade 7 Teacher

How might I encourage students to slow down and take a look at words they are reading in their novels? What activity might I introduce that would have students make careful choices about using words? I thought blackout poetry would be an appropriate activity with students who were developing skills in two areas: jot note-taking for science and descriptive creative writing. As disparate as these two skills sets are, they both emphasize word choice and economy of communication. I wanted my students to be able identify and isolate the key words of a text, in this case a two-paragraph descriptive passage from a novel of their choice, while preserving the essence of the source material in terms of meaning, function, and mood.

We had already been working on writing tasks that involved describing famous works of art; i.e., *describe this painting as accurately and objectively as you can* and *describe this painting using heightened and poetic language.* Students were then asked to find a two-paragraph passage that they felt were strong examples of descriptive writing in their current favorite book. After some discussion, they concluded that strong descriptive writing formed pictures in their minds by creating clear images with just the right combination of nouns, verbs, adjectives, and adverbs.

Armed with markers, they were asked to black out words and phrases from their photocopied passages until they were left with the barest minimum of words. One of the keys to this activity, as with the jot note-taking skills they had been developing, was to keep only what was necessary. I likened it to packing for a holiday: They didn't want to fill their suitcases too heavily and get weighed down, nor did they want to be left unprepared by bringing too little. Once they felt they found the right balance, they were ready to share what was left with their peers who would then guess what was communicated in the original text. Before adapting the remaining text into a free-verse poem, students revised their blackouts based on this feedback.

One of the challenges they encountered was determining how much of the text they could black out. The initial impulse for many was to be cautious with the marker and leave too many phrases intact. With encouragement, many were able to separate the important words from rest. They learned to select the smallest number of words that communicated the most. The most successful students were able to appreciate the power of brevity in their final free-verse poems by being highly selective and thoughtful about the words they chose.

Beautiful Woods
by: Liam PS

Beautiful Woods,
Lush And Green,
snow fell Like Glitter,
branches curve under the snow,
Bowing
And
Twisting
in the
Wind,

Inspired by The Marrow Thieves by Cherie Dimaline

Using Poem Snippets

As suggested in Appreciating Novel Words (page 73), students can consider lines from a poem that they find intriguing. Looking at two or three lines from a poem in isolation as snippets encourages lingering over words and taking a microscopic look at how words are carefully considered by a poet.

Snippets can be

- displayed throughout the classroom for others to ponder
- a source for illustration, using an art medium of choice
- recorded as a piece of graffiti (accompanied by poet's name) to create a wall mural for others to examine. Snippets can be from a favorite poet, or based on a theme.
- hidden inside a poem. The challenge is to add a thought before or after the snippet (or both before and after) to create a new poem. Poems can be rhymed; however, the result may be more playful if the poem is in free-verse form.

The following short snippet samples are fragments from longer poems students have written.

Poems are like barbecued steaks
Sometimes tender
Sometimes juicy
Sometimes
well done
— Liza

The earth is like a diamond
So hard to break
— Matt

Onions, relish, tomatoes ripe
Mustard, lettuce, a ketchup stripe
— Alan

I want to go home
But I have to do a poem
— Jamie

Poor little bird,
Alone like me
Both without our mothers.
— Sara

Dotted butterfly
Flutters by
Way up high
— Samantha

A rich red ruby
Zooms on by
(cardinal)
— Erik

My dog's
tongue Is a
silky wet
blanket
— Andrea

I am pouncing paws
I am silent leap
I am cat
— Sarah

A bird without wings
Is like a book without a reader
—Rachael

The snail creeps upon the ground
Watching others hurry.
— Jeffrey

But the best chips
Are friend chips!
— Natasha

Exploring Poetic Forms

I have some hesitation in recommending poem writing according to a formula. Poetry is not always a paint-by-numbers exercise in which we fill in spaces according to rules. When students are working as poets, we need to help them experiment with a varied palette, using the kind of word paint that they wish—and feeling free to go outside the lines. However, writing poems from a model can be a good way to begin writing poetry. Teaching poetic forms helps students choose and use words by having them

- play with patterns
- count syllables
- comply with a specific metre or rhythm
- explore rhyme
- eliminate unnecessary words
- rearrange the order of words
- replace words with "better" choices
- investigate words (using dictionary, thesaurus, etc.)

Examples by Sheree Fitch first appeared in *The Poetry Experience* by Sheree Fitch and Larry Swartz.

Some Poetic Forms

Acrostic

- first letter of each line spells out the subject of the poem
- for every letter in the word, a word or group of words tells about the subject

> **P**erfect words
> **O**rganized with care
> **E**nchant your ear
> **T**ransform your worlds

Refresh
Your heart
— Sheree Fitch

Haiku

- contains three unrhymed lines
- usually 17 syllables arranged in lines of 5–7–5 syllables
- most often describes scenes in nature

> In the field, a deer
> I blink once, he disappears,
> Overhead, crows laugh
> — Sheree Fitch

> By a frozen lake
> A jay darts to take quick flight
> Blue sky flash over ice
> — Christi, age 11

Cinquain

- pronounced "SING-kane"
- five lines in length
- often composed of a set number of syllables
- common model: one word/two adjectives/three *-ing* words/four words about the subject/fifth line can repeat first line

> Saturday
> Peaceful morning
> Lingering over breakfast
> Quiet joy in writing time
> Freedom
> — Sheree Fitch

> Werewolf
> Scary, Hairy
> Howling, Yowling, Prowling
> Beware the stalker's bite
> Werewolf
> — Erica, age 11

Limerick

- five-line poem
- AABBA rhyme scheme
- usually humorous
- bouncy rhythm

> There once was a dancer named Clive
> Who danced a hot salsa and jive
> Until one night he tripped
> He slid and he slipped
> Now he's twisted but staying alive.
> — Sheree Fitch

For more on list poems, see pages 59–62.

List Poem

- a list of words about a topic or subject
- there is a link or a pattern; e.g. all words are adjectives, verbs, or alliterative words
- does not have to rhyme

> One baby skunk
> One sister skunk
> One brother skunk
> One father skunk
> One mother skunk
> One grandma skunk
> One grandpa skunk
> STUNK!
> — Larry Swartz

Rhyming Couplet

- two-line poem (or stanza) that rhymes
- when a complete poem is made, is considered a "closed couplet"

> If I were a bird and a bird was me
> He'd be writing this poem and I'd be up a tree.
> — Larry Swartz

Three-Word Model

- a noun, a verb, an adverb (in that order)
- words are listed vertically
- use of alliteration to give the poem a unifying link

> raccoons rummage rowdily
> — Alex, age 10

Quatrain

- the most common stanza in English poetry
- made up of four lines
- usually rhymed AABB, ABAB, or ABCB

> There were monkeys in my kitchen
> They were climbing up the walls
> They were dancing on the ceiling
> They were bouncing basketballs
> — Sheree Fitch

Responding to Poetry Using the Written Word

What the reader brings to a text is part of the construction of the literary experience. The finding of meanings, according to response theorist Louise Rosenblatt, involves both the author's text and what the reader brings to it. We need to make a strong effort to recognize each individual response to a poem, not only because the response reveals something about the thinking and culture of the reader, but because we will be helping readers to discover the meaning of poetry—the power of poem words—for themselves.

When we provide time and structure for students to respond to a poem, we are encouraging them to take a magnifying glass to a poem's words and a telescope to the big-idea meaning behind those words. The more we help our students become familiar with personal response, the more apt they might be to share their thoughts and opinions about any text. When we meet with others to explore a poem's meanings we can discuss

- the content of the poem
- the theme of the poem
- the poet's intent
- the title
- the stories within the poem
- puzzlements and wonderings (questions)
- the choice of words by the poet, including rhyme scheme
- the shape and form of the poem on the page
- personal connections to the poem
- how the poem makes us feel

Short poems like the one presented here have served me well in helping students understand that their response is personal and their opinions matter:

> Cloud comes
> Drinks up the sea,
> And spits on me.
> — Jenny Nelson from *Island Rhymes*

Students begin by writing a response and then work in small groups with their peers, which helps them recognize that there are a range of responses to a text, some similar to their own, others quite different.

> I like the poem because it is short and tells a story in a few words, making you think. — Clive

> I don't understand how the cloud drinks up the sea. Clouds can't drink. — Zachary

> This poem makes me think about rain, the sea, taking a shower, drinking water, washing dishes, water balloons, wetting my hair and falling in a puddle. — Max

> The cloud is like a person because people drink and clouds don't really don't. — Joshua

> This poet must like rain even when it 'spits'. I like the use of that word because it paints a picture of how the cloud sends water to the earth. — Samantha

> The poet makes picture of the rain falling gently from the sky. — Tara

> This poem reminds me of yesterday. It rained and I was supposed to go camping. I just stayed inside and played video games. When the rain stopped, I went to my friend's house and we went roller blading. — Bryan

There are a number of ways students can share their written responses to poems that they meet when reading independently or that are introduced by the teacher. If reading response journals are used in your program, students can record some of their thoughts as they would about any piece of text. They can also respond on a separate piece of paper or, even better, a file card because it invites students to be succinct.

Most responses will be recorded after students have read the poem, though in some cases they may respond to a poem's title, or record some of their thoughts and questions as they read the poem line by line, word by word. Written responses can be shared with teacher or peers. Further learning can arise when students share their writing in small or large groups and discover that what they have written may be similar or different from what others have thought. Sometimes written responses can be facilitated following a discussion about the poem. This allows students to reflect on what has been said and to articulate what they have taken from the poem and/or the discussion.

The more familiar students become with personal response, the more apt they are to share their thoughts and opinions about a text and come to recognize that responses are personal and valid. Though students are encouraged to respond to a poem in any way, at times they might need some thinking stems (I wonder…, I remember…, I feel…) or questions to guide their response.

Ten Questions to Guide a Student's Response to a Poem

1. In one sentence, what is the poem about?
2. What is it about the poem that you particularly liked? Disliked?
3. What did the poem remind you of?
4. What things in the poem did you see? Hear? Feel? Taste?
5. Did this poem give you special feelings? Explain.
6. Is the title of the poem truthful? Might you suggest an alternative title?
7. What are some questions or wonderings you have about the poem?
8. How is this poem different or similar to other poems you have read?
9. What would you tell or ask the poet about the poem?
10. How is this a poem?

Bonus about Words: What one word, two words, or group of words did you find to be interesting or powerful? Explain.

Bookshelf: Recent Poetry Anthologies.

Ages 7+.

Kwame Alexander; photographs by Joel Sartore. *Animal Ark*
Nicola Davies; illus. Petr Horáček. *Song of the Wild: A first book of animals*
Sheree Fitch; illus. Darcia Labrosse. *If You Could Wear My Sneakers* (20th anniversary edition)
Sheree Fitch & Anne Hunt. *Whispers of Mermaids and Wonderful Things: Children's poetry and verse from Atlantic Canada*
Chris Harris; illus. Lane Smith. *I'm Just No Good at Rhyming: and other nonsense for mischievous kids and immature grown-ups*
Robert Macfarlane; illus. Jackie Morris. *The Lost Words*
Amy Ludwig VanDerwater; illus. Ryan O'Rourke. *Read! Read! Read!*

Ages 12+

Kwame Alexander (with Chris Colderley and Marjory Wentworth) (eds.) *Out of Wonder: Poems celebrating poets*
Brian Bilston. *You Took the Last Bus Home*
David Booth; illus. Maya Ishiura. *Bird Guy*
David Bouchard; paintings by Dennis J. Weber. *Proud to be Métis*

Nikki Grimes. *One Last Word*
Naomi Shihab Nye. *Voices in the Air: Poems for Listeners*

Resources for Teaching Poetry

Kwame Alexander. *The Write Thing: Kwame Alexander Engages Students in Writing Workshop (and you can too!)*
David Booth & Bill Moore. *Poems Please: Sharing Poetry with Children*
David Booth & Bob Barton. *Poetry Goes to School*
Sheree Fitch & Larry Swartz. *The Poetry Experience: Choosing and Using Poetry in the Classroom*
Amy Ludwig VanDerwater. *Poems are Teachers*

"Oral reading verifies print and helps silent readers to 'hear' dialogue." (Booth, 2013)

Lifting the Words Off the Page

There are many opportunities, inside and outside the classroom, for students to gain practice in rehearsing and presenting words from a page, and by doing so they are digging deeper into the meaning behind those words. David Booth has suggested the term *rehearsed talk* for talk influenced by print. In rehearsed talk, students are reading the words from a page through opportunities that allow them to lift those words off the page, to bring meaning to those words through voice, expression, and gesture, and thus to come to understand the reciprocal nature of speaker and listener. Students usually find that reading aloud—especially after rehearsing the text—is a satisfying mode of communication. By focusing on the words, they find that pronunciation and meaning enhance their reading comprehension skills as they consider ways to present text to an audience, small or large.

In the classroom, there are several opportunities for rehearsed, scripted talk by students working alone or in small groups, visiting and revisiting words on the page and therefore becoming better aware of the subtext, the layer of meaning, the associations of the words that lie below the surface. Students can

- Make announcements
- Read aloud a picture book (e.g., to a peer, to a younger audience, to a buddy)
- Report information they have researched
- Make a public speech
- Give instructions (e.g., a game, a science experiment, a math problem)
- Read their own writing
- Read jokes and riddles
- Share a favorite poem, novel excerpt, or piece of nonfiction text
- Rehearse and present readers theatre
- Rehearse and present scripts (including monologues)
- Rehearse and present poems through choral dramatization

Poems Aloud: Choral Dramatization

When we read a poem on a page, the words are nothing more than black ink on white paper. When a poem is read aloud, we can make it come to life through our voice. In choral dramatization, student work with others (in pairs, small groups, whole class). Groups are given a copy of a poem and are challenged to read it together in the manner of their choice, experimenting with voice, gesture, and presentation. The process of choral dramatization demands that students pay careful attention to the words—and the intent—of the poet.

When our students read poems aloud, their eyes and ears are exploring the rhythms of language, the sounds of words. When done well, oral interpretation can improve comprehension skills, helping students to come to grips with all the meanings to which the words give rise. One measure of understanding a poem comes from the way the poem is recited. Working with a poem's words until they flow from the tongue with meaning and understanding is the true test of how well it is read.

Choral speaking invites students to read aloud such texts as rhymes and poems by assigning parts among group members. By working with peers to read aloud poems on a particular theme or topic, or by a single poet, students take part in a creative activity that involves experimentation with voice, sound, gesture, and movement. Because of these variations, no two oral interpretations of a single poem are alike. When students read and rehearse poems to present to others, the poet's intent must be internalized, so that the reader becomes familiar with the flavor of the words, their cadence and their flow.

Choral speaking enhances skills of reading aloud and presentation. When students work in small groups to read aloud together, their problem-solving skills are likely to be enriched as they make decisions about the way to present a poem. Choral speaking is a unique and engaging way for students to inspect words. Not only are they using a meaningful context for pronouncing words but they are bringing meaning to each word through their voices. How words are said out loud, pausing and pacing, using pitch and tone, encourages students to animate print, to lift words off the page.

Ways to Read Poems Aloud

Some poems, like this one by Sonja Dunn, are perfect for choral speaking, with cues for oral presentation right in the poem.

Listen to the Rain
by Sonja Dunn
Listen, listen
Listen to the rain
Listen, listen,
Listen to the rain

Softer, softer
Listen to the rain
Softer, softer,
Listen to the rain

Louder, louder
Listen to the rain.
Louder, louder
Listen to the rain.

Listen, listen
Listen to the rain
Listen, listen, listen, listen
Listen to the rain

Another rain poem, "Sound of Water" by Mary O'Neill, offers possibilities for reading aloud in a variety of ways. As students suggest sounds for each word, the poem enhances their understanding of onomatopoeia (from the Greek; imitates, resembles, or suggests the sound that a word describes).

Sound of Water
> by Mary O'Neill

The sound of water is
Rain,
Lap,
Fold,
Slap,
Gurgle,
Splash,
Churn,
Crash,
Murmur,
Pour,
Ripple,
Roar,
Plunge,
Drip,
Spout,
Skip,
Sprinkle,
Flow,
Ice,
Snow.

The following are suggested strategies for reading these rain poems chorally:
- Reading in unison.
- Reading the poem quickly.
- Reading from slow to fast, from fast to slow.
- Reading from loud to soft, from soft to loud.
- Group 1 reads from the top to bottom; group 2 from bottom to top.
- Teacher reads the lines; students make the sounds that the words suggest.
- Teacher reads the lines; students do a hand gesture to interpret to the words.
- Teacher reads one line, group alternates lines.
- Teacher reads lines; students echo the way the teacher reads the words.
- Reading cumulatively with each person, in turn, joining in.
- Students are divided into 2 or 3 groups and the poem is read as a round.
- Students are individually assigned words and the entire poem is read aloud.
- Students, standing, add a gesture or movement to accompany their word.

Extension

Students can work in groups to create their own list poems by brainstorming words on a particular topic: Sound of School, Sound of Winter, Sound of Summer; Sound of Sports. Encourage students to make decisions about ways to arrange words; for example, by syllables, just verbs, or repeating words. Students can work with group members to rehearse and present their invented poem chorally.

Reading Aloud in Small Groups

An alternative way to work with poetry is to provide each group with the same poem. Though the text is the same for each group, the presentations will be diverse, depending on how each group manipulates the poem, using choral techniques.

Students are arranged into groups of three to five. Each group is assigned a poem on the topic of rain to read chorally. To begin, students collaborate to divide the lines amongst group members, deciding which parts might be said in unison, in groups, in pairs, individually. Once students have practiced several ways to say the words of the poem aloud, have them decide on actions and/or sounds to accompany each line.

Ways to Choose Poems

- Use poems from an anthology by a single poet.
- Use poems on a single theme or topic; e.g., Peace, Friendship, Food, Bullying, Animals, Nature, etc.
- Use a longer poem, with each group exploring one or two verses of that poem.

Bookshelf: Out-Loud Poetry.

Maya Angelou; illus. Jean-Michel Basquiat. *Life Doesn't Frighten Me*
David Booth. *Head to Toe Spaghetti and Other Tasty Rhymes*
David Booth & Larry Swartz (eds.). *The Bully, The Bullied, The Bystander, The Brave*
Wade & Cheryl Willis Hudson (eds.) *We Rise, We Resist, We Raise Our Voices*
Sonja Dunn. *All Together Now*
Sheree Fitch. *Toes in My Nose* (also *Everybody's Different on Different Street*)
Douglas Florian. *Laugh-eteria*
Nikki Giovanni. *Hip Hop Speaks to Children: A celebration of poetry with a beat.*
Dennis Lee. *Bubblegum Delicious* (also *Alligator Pie, Garbage Delight, The Ice Cream Store, Jelly Belly*)

7

What Does That Mean?

"When I use a word," Humpty Dumpty said, in a rather scornful tone, "it means what I choose it to mean—neither more nor less."

"The question is," said Alice, "whether you can make words mean so many different things."

"The question is," said Humpty Dumpty, "which is to be the master—that's all."

— from *Through the Looking Glass* by Lewis Carroll

Vowels and consonants sit alongside each other to form a word that is a symbol of meaning. Our students need a way into the world of big words, small words, old words, new words, familiar words, strange words, words from our own culture, and words from the cultures of others. They need to hear, talk about, read, reread, write, explore, and experiment with print to develop and internalize literacy strategies. Providing opportunities for students to dig deeper into the meaning of words helps them to expand their knowledge and understanding of words, perhaps increasing their word smarts.

A single word can mean many different things, determined by the contact of the print or of the conversation, the purpose or function of its use, and, especially, the background and life experience of the reader. Watching a documentary about the life of Leonard Bernstein prompted me to look up the meaning of the word *mixolydian* and learn that is a musical mode or scale. In my lifetime, I'm not likely to use the word *mixolydian*, but looking up the meaning helped me to understand what was being demonstrated in a music class. In writing about etymology in this chapter, I was curious about its meaning. I knew that a word ending in the suffix *–ology* means that the word is a field of study. Researching the word *etymology* informed me that the origin of the word comes from the Greek word *etymon* meaning "literal meaning of a word according to its origin," and is not to be confused with *entomology*, the student of insects. When a student told me that her name was Miruna, I asked her if she knew what her name meant and was told it's from *mir*, a Romanian word for a herb that is burnt in orthodox churches to bring on feelings of peace.

Our classrooms can provide a culture that lets students to find the derivation of the word, the culture of the word, and its varied meaning in varied forms. Encouraging our students to be word detectives helps them use print and online references to discover what words mean and gain information about words to understand their etymology and their use in time and place. It is also important to note, as Mark Weakland points out, that "if we can deeply teach students the meaning of their spelling words, then we are building their vocabulary even as we teach sound and letter recognition" (Weakland, 2017, p. 70). Wondering about the meaning of words builds a curiosity about words and helps students to find a place for those words in their lives.

When we invite students to look at the origin of words, it not only enhances their understanding of the English language, but provides them with insights into their roots with articles. When we look up a word in a print or online dictionary, information about the derivation of a word is given to help us understand the birth and development of a word. Helping students to think etymologically can

- spark curiosity and inquiry
- enhance word knowledge
- help understand and apply spelling concepts
- enrich historical thinking

In this chapter students will have opportunities to

- Find meaning and tell and write stories about their names
- Recount and tell personal stories drawn from a single word
- Consider words that are archaic
- Notice and celebrate words that are particular to the 21st century
- Understand how words are borrowed from other languages
- Consider our differences by discussing and reflecting on when words can be hurtful
- Expand their word knowledge by considering politically correct terminology

Names and Meaning

"There is nobody on earth with the same name as me. I am the only Thunder Boy who has ever lived."
— Sherman Alexie, *Thunder Boy Jr.*

For most of us, the first word we hear is our names. Everyone has a name. Everyone has a story about his or her name. Belarie Zatzman, Associate Dean at York University, has conducted research on names as artifacts of our identities:

Have you ever thought about your name and what it says about you? The connection between identity and how we represent ourselves can begin to be explored through our names, which serve as markers of our identity. In many cultures, names are very significant to help us understand where a person is from, who his/ her ancestors are, or what type of qualities the family hopes that child will possess. The United Nations Convention on the Rights of the Child states that every child has the right to a name and an identity. (in Swartz, 2010, p. 12)

Students can tell or write stories about their names by considering the following prompts:

- Who, if anybody, were you named after?
- What does your name mean?

- Does your name have a history in your family?
- Do you know your name in other languages?
- Do you have a nickname?
- Are you fond of your name?
- What name would you choose for yourself, if given a choice?
- What is an interesting (e.g., funny, sad, embarrassing, frustrating) story that involves your name?
- How do you think your first and/or last name influences your identity?

These names stories emerged from Ahren Sternberg's Grades 5/6 classroom:

> My name is Mia and I love it! My parents were going to name me Summer because I was born on the summer solstice. I'm glad they named me Mia.

> My name is Georgia. In Latin it means "farmer's daughter." My parents chose the name because my dad LOVES music (me too!). When my mom was thinking of girl names, she thought of Georgia and of course my dad loved it because of that jazzy song "Georgia on My Mind."

> My mom and dad named me Jeremy. Before I was born they each prepared a list with three names on it. Both of them had the name Jeremy on the list.

> Believe it or not, I wasn't given a name for the first month of my life until my father decided to put an ad in the paper asking people for suggestions. My father's John. His father was John. My uncle was John. My mother is Irish, so my name, Ian, is an Irish version of John.

> Once upon a time there was a kid blessed by God, and thus was born Adam.

In the Classroom: Names and Personal Narratives
by Heather Brandes, Grade 7 Teacher

At the start of this school year, my Grade 7 students used the literary text, *Thunderboy Jr.* by Sherman Alexie to begin to examine their unique personal narratives and social identities. Leading up to our culminating activity, the students played many name games to become familiar with one another and to start to build an inclusive community within the classroom. The picture book was read aloud to students and I stopped midway at the pivotal line where the main character pronounces, "I hate my name!"; I felt it provided a spark for students to consider what they liked about their names. Students were then provided with a list of reflection questions about their names and were asked to respond in writing to the list of questions designed to help them think about their names and stories connected to their names.

In the next phase of the lesson, students worked in groups of two or to share responses prompted by their written answers. Students revealed personal narratives that were drawn from their experiences, their memories, their family histories, and their emotional connections. As I listened to their stories, I found them to be fascinating, powerful, and authentic.

The small-group discussion inspired me to create a community circle where each student shared their story. The circle sharing was a rich opportunity for listening and speaking. Moreover, the sharing of name stories provided a meaningful context for the students to build trust, insight, and understanding in one another. Some students who had been together since Kindergarten were overheard saying, "I never knew that about you!" Names were shared in many languages, such as Tamil, Vietnamese, Hebrew, and Bengali, and feelings of pride, joy, and excitement were evident in many of the personal narratives. All students willingly supported one another with total concentration, active engagement, and genuine appreciation, while their peers bravely shared their social identities.

The oral narratives seemed to well prepare the students to write their stories. They were given the following questions to think about: How do our names reflect who we are? How do our names relate to our identities? What characteristics are reflected in your name and in your identity?

Students were given large pieces of square paper and were asked to illustrate their written ideas using the shape of a spiral. The innermost line of the spiral was the beginning of their story. The spiral shape was chosen to visually represent the students' personal journeys and their "ripple in the world." The spiral reminded some students of their fingerprint; others thought it represented how they started off small and developed throughout the years, and how their identities have a limitless opportunity to continue to grow. All artwork was displayed in our classroom and students frequently visited the bulletin board to continue reading about one another. Sharing our social identities this way genuinely helped to develop a strong sense of community and belonging within our classroom. The work created was culturally relevant and reflective of the students that I teach. The lesson began with one word—our names. Each of us has a name; each of us has a story.

Bookshelf: Books Featuring Names

Sherman Alexie; illus. Yuyi Morales. *Thunder Boy Jr.*
Joseph Bruchac; illus. Rocco Baviera. *A Boy Called Slow*
Yangsook Choi. *The Name Jar*
Kevin Henkes. *Chrysanthemum*
Helen Recorvits; illus Gabi Swiatkowska. *My Name is Yoon*
Laura Vaccaro Seeger. *Walter Was Worried*
Karen Lynn Williams & Khadra Mohammed; illus. Catherine Stock. *My Name is Sangoel*

Name Aerobics

Students write their first names on a sheet or card as an acrostic. For each letter of the name, a verb or phrase is chosen or an exercise movement is described.

JOSHUA
J = Jump high
O = Overhead stretch
S = Swing arms
H = Hug yourself
U = Under and over
A = Arm lifts

Students practice a routine by performing each of the exercises in their names. They can find a partner, exchange cards, and learn the routine outlined on their partner's sheet.

Extension: Students work in groups of five or six. Each person has a chance to be the leader, instructing others about the routines by calling out the verbs or phrases associated with their names. Each routine can be repeated three to five times.

Name Scrabble

Give each student sticky notes, one for each letter of their first name. Students write each letter in their first name on a note. Students scramble letters in their first names to make as many words as possible; for example, Deborah could derive the words *bed*, *dear*, *read*, and *heard* from her name. When students have exhausted all possibilities, they team up with a partner. Combining letters from both names, they make as many words as possible.

Extensions

- Students work in groups of three or four to make words using the letters from all their first names.
- Students repeat the activity using their first and last names.

Every Word a Story

"Children are wise, but they don't know how wise. And sometimes they don't have words for what they know."
— from *My Father's Words* by Patricia MacLachlan

The stories of our lives are swimming inside our heads. When we talk with others, these stories pop out of our mouths from the human need to share them with others. When we are at parties, at family gatherings, at mealtime, in the hallways of school, or at a mall, we tell stories. Usually, there is no specific prompt for sharing these memories. Sometimes a book, a movie, or a news report reminds us of things that happened to us. Often when others tell their stories, ours are awakened, and when we are comfortable with the people we are with, we choose to tell these stories.

Teachers and their students have a treasure chest of stories waiting to be unlocked and shared. When students tell personal stories, they are not only choosing to reveal their life experiences to others, but they are also building a dimension of who they are. Sometimes when a topic is offered in classrooms, students may not be able to make an immediate personal connection, but they can be encouraged to tell stories about someone they know or have read about.

Personal narratives can emerge from

- children's literature shared in class: "*Dog* by Matthew Van Fleet is a story about a dog. Does anyone have a dog, or know someone who has a dog? What other pet stories might you have?"

- a topic or question
- a story shared by someone else: "Your story reminds me of the time…"
- an artifact; e.g., a photograph, a toy, an article of clothing, etc.
- a word; e.g., seashore, stitches, surprise, celebration, prize, costume, etc.

From Word to Story

Word prompts can be offered to the students to inspire personal narrative:

Nouns	Emotions	Issues
contest	sad	racism
accident	excited	classism
robbery	relieved	ableism
beach	thrilled	homophobia
embarrassment	anxious	immigration
museum	afraid	bullying
vacation	nervous	cyberbullying

Sharing Personal Narratives

As an alternative, members of the group can choose a word from a list you have provided that inspires a personal narrative.

For this activity, students work in groups of three or four to tell anecdotes or stories of things they have experienced. Members of the group can decide on one topic from a suggested list. A volunteer begins by telling their story to others. Students are encouraged to provide as much detail as possible about the event and be prepared to answer questions from group members. Each member of the group should have the opportunity to share a story.

Telling/Retelling/Retelling in Role

- Students work in pairs, each telling a story.
- As a follow-up, students find a new partner and retell the story they just heard (i.e., their first partner's story).
- The activity can be extended by having students find another new partner. This time the first partner's story is told in the first person. Storytellers tell the story as if it were their own, using the pronoun *I*, telling the story in role.

That Reminds Me

Provide a list of suggested topics to small groups of students. Each group decides on a topic to begin a conversation about personal experiences. One person is chosen to be the leader and tells a story. When this person completes their story, other group members raise their hand and say, "That reminds me…" if a word or incident mentioned by the first storyteller inspires a story. The activity continues with each member volunteering to share an anecdote when reminded of one from another person's story.

From Telling to Writing

Following oral storytelling, students are encouraged to write a personal narrative that can serve as a record for the events of their lives. The out-loud storytelling, whether to a partner, a small group, or the whole class, serves as a rehearsal, a preparation for writing the story rooted by a single word.

In his book *Writing Radar: Using Your Journal to Snoop Out and Craft Great Stories*, Newbery Medal Winner Jack Gantos offers two very useful lists of key words that can lead to oral and written narrative.

Key Words That Lead to Ideas for Action in a Story:
brothers, sisters, parents, sleepovers, triumphs, disasters, chores, pets, camping, etc. (Gantos, 2017, pp. 96–97)

Key Words That Lead to Ideas for Emotions in a Story:
defeated, stunned, bored, frustrated, inferior, confused, disillusioned, enthusiastic, brave, curious, anxious, afraid, neglected, hopeless, grumpy, worried, awkward, insulted, cheerful, proud, content, amused, tender, helpless, dread, powerless, bitter, relaxed, loved, trusting, humiliated, pity (Gantos, 2017, pp. 99–100)

Six-Word Memoirs

Ernest Hemingway was once asked to write a full story that contained only six words and he came up with this: "For Sale: baby shoes, never worn."

Six-Word Memoirs is a project founded by Smith Magazine, a U.S. online publication that provides a platform for storytelling in many forms. In 2006, Smith editors Larry Smith and Rachel Fershleiser asked readers to submit their life story in just six-words:

Kid gets magic set, pursues dream. —Gerry K.
One box of tissues wasn't enough. — Neha J.
Peer pressure made me do it. — Marlene V.
I never believed this would happen. — Kailey Z.
This time, I actually hit send. — Naomi T.
(Smith & Fershleiser, 2009)

Students can be challenged to distill stories from their own lives into exactly six words. Funny, sad, succinct, or puzzling, six-word memoirs can serve as a synthesis of life experiences or as a seed for more elaborate personal narratives.

Yesterday's Words

"Words die out when they are no longer at the heart of our language."
— Nick Enfield, professor of linguistics, Sydney University

When is a word considered archaic? The term *archaic* is used for words that were once common but are now rarely used; e.g., *jargogle* (to confuse or jumble), *corrade* (to scrape together), or *kench* (to laugh loudly).

When is a word considered obsolete? *Obsolete* may apply to a word that is regarded as no-longer acceptable or useful, even though it is still in existence; e.g., *hath* (has), *doth* (do), *nay* (no), *ye* (you).

About 1000 new words are added to the dictionary each year: recent examples include *selfie* and *hashtag*. However, over time, there are thousands of words that can become passé, obsolete, extinct, or archaic because they have under-utilized. When was the last time you used (or heard someone use) *thou* or *methinks* or *fortnight* in everyday conversation? Are the words *groovy* or *cool* still groovy or cool, i.e., popular in our everyday language?

Some words attract lots of interest at certain times but can also get dated really quickly because they aren't relevant. Words can become obsolete because

- The thing that they refer to no longer exists; e.g., *boombox*, *floppy disk*
- Fashionable terms become unused and replaced by others;. e.g., *bosom buddy* becomes *bestie*
- Words can be superseded by other ways of communicating, like emojis

Ask students: Are these words at risk of being endangered (if they aren't already)?

laptop	trend
CD	fax
dude	cheque
bestie	woke

Becoming a Lexicographer

Students meet in groups of five or six. Each is assigned a word that is considered obsolete (see list below). Students take on the role of dictionary editors who have been hired to decide which words will be eliminated in the newly published dictionary. As a lexicographer, each student is challenged to persuade others that their word should be included. They will need to explain the meaning of the word, perhaps giving sentences to help explain the meaning. As an alternative, students prioritize the words from most to least significant for today's world.

This list is compiled from 30 Amazing, Intriguing, Obsolete Words We Should Absolutely Start Using Again: https://expresswriters.com/amazing-obsolete-words-in-the-english-dictionary/

- brabble: to argue over something that's not very important
- curmuring: when your stomach gives a loud rumbling because you are hungry
- gorgonize: to have a mesmerizing effect on someone
- groak: to watch someone eat silently as they eat, in the hope that you will be invited to join them
- grumpish (1720s): similar to being sullen or grumpy or cranky
- houppelande: a type of cloak worn in medieval times
- monsterful (1810s): something extraordinary or wonderful
- sluberdegullion: a slovenly, lazy person (i.e., a couch potato)
- snowbrowth (1590s): freshly melted snow
- twattle: to gossip

Other obsolete words to investigate:

apricity	grok
boondoggle	hugger-mugger
elflock	zenzizenzizenzic

Awesome Words of the 21st Century

"A word is not a crystal, transparent and unchanging, it is the skin of a living thought and may vary greatly in color and content according to the circumstances and time in which it is used."
— Oliver Wendell Holmes, Jr.

Can you remember when *tweet* was a sound a bird made and *wrap* something we did to presents? Can you remember when *salty* was a way to describe food, *woke* was something you did in the morning, and *chill* described something cold?

Words may come and words may go, but living in modern times challenges us to keep up with all that's new, and that includes English vocabulary. Words may emerge from TV and movies, e.g., *bazinga*, from *The Big Bang Theory*, *fetch* from *Mean Girls*, *d'oh* from *The Simpsons*; from music (*rap*, *funk*), or from popular culture (*hoodie*, *grunge*, *goth*). Some words may get borrowed from the language of other cultures: e.g., *paparazzi*, *cappuccino* (Italian); *macho*, *cucaracha* (Spanish). Many common words that emerge or change from recent technology—*social media*, *Twitter*, *app*, *Uber*—were likely not part of everyday lingo a decade or so ago, even though they had meanings used in contexts different from their use today.

The familiarity of phrases used every day are given legitimacy by appearing on Oxford's online dictionary (not to be confused with the hardcopy version of the Oxford English Dictionary). In fact, Oxford updates their web collection of words every three months. Though we might hope that usage is consistent across generations, some words are born from and connected to youth culture. Each year, Oxford University Press monitors hundreds of new words and expressions and adds popular words to its official list, allowing words we invent or repurpose to become recognized as "real." In order to appear in the print dictionary, a word must remain significant for a period of two or three years; however, digitally, a word's currency can be for a much shorter period of time. According to Global Language Monitor, about 5400 new words are created every year. About 1000 new words are deemed worth entering into the dictionary because of their significant widespread use.

> It is worth noting that many words have roots in urban culture with specific meanings and history (e.g., *nappy*, *gangsta*, *squad*, *savage*). If someone isn't Black and uses the lingo, is it a form of cultural appropriation, or just an indication that Black, or urban, culture is cool?

Discussing 21st-Century Words

Consider these five words recently added to the Oxford Dictionary:

> *Meh*: Expressing a lack of interest
> *Selfie*: A photograph taken by yourself on a smart phone and then most often shared on social media
> *Emoji*: A small icon used to show emotion digitally
> *Yolo*: Acronym for the phrase You Only Live Once
> *Bitcoin*: An electronic currency that can be transferred securely without the need of a bank to regulate it
> *Twitter*: A social media website

- Which of these six words do you think is still popular today?
- Which of these six words is the least popular today?
- Which of these words do you think will eventually become obsolete?
- Which of these words, if any, have you used in your writing?
- What are some new words that have been part of our culture in the past two years?

> Many nouns are generated by adding the –*ie* suffix or –*y* suffix; e.g., *freebie*, *foodie*, *newbie*, *roomie*, *scrunchie*.

Extension

Look at more examples of new words. Will these words soon be obsolete? Are they already?

> *Fuhgeddaboudit*: "Forget about it" using a New Jersey or New York accent, meaning "It's not going to happen"
> *millennial*: a person reaching adulthood in the early 21st century
> *tweenager*: a child between the ages of 10 and 14

fake news: supposed to describe completely inaccurate and fabricated news, but is now commonly used to describe any news that goes against one's views

crowdfunding: the practice of funding a project or business venture by raising many small amounts of money from a large number of people

grunge: subculture of alternative rock music; a type of comfortable, often dirty, flannel clothing that was popular in that music scene

photobomb: a photograph that has been spoiled by the unexpected appearance of an object or person in the camera's field of view just as the picture was taken; usually a prank or joke

Text Messaging Words

gr8 Texting Words Answers:
 1. tomorrow
 2. Before You Know It
 3. Be Right There
 4. sleepy
 5. Can't Talk Now
 6. See You Soon
 7. Easy as 1, 2, 3
 8. Face to Face
 9. Fingers Crossed
10. Friend Of A Friend
11. Hugs And Kisses
12. Just Kidding
13. Just To Let You Know
14. Okay (not sarcastic)
15. No Comment
16. No Problem
17. Never Mind
18. On A Totally Unrelated Subject
19. On My Way
20. On The Phone
21. Right Now
22. Still In The Dark
23. Welcome Back
24. Will You Call Me?
25. Wish You Were Here

Any discussion about words in the 21st century needs to highlight the use of text messaging or texting, an informal, efficient, and highly popular way of electronically communicating messages where brevity is expected and accepted. Youth and adults alike use text messages for personal, family, business, and social purposes andithas become an accepted part of many cultures. New forms of interaction that were not possible before are now made possible with the advent of text messaging. People can carry out conversations with others without the constraints of an expected reply within a short amount of time and without needing to set time aside to engage in conversation. Drawing attention to text messaging in the classroom can help students understand how this mode of communication is positive and helpful or negative and challenging to our understanding of words and how we communicate.

Have students alone or with a partner to complete the gr8 Texting Words test on page 124 to test their knowledge of text messaging abbreviations.

Teaching Tips

Text messaging mostly appears as abbreviations or acronyms and visual icons. To help students understand the differences, explain:

- An abbreviation is a shortened form of a word or phrase used mainly in writing to represent the complete form: e.g., St./street; approx./ approximately.
- An acronym is a pronounceable word formed mostly (not always) from the initial letters of a name or title: e.g., ASAP/As soon as possible; FYI/For Your Information.
- Ideograms, aka emoticons or emojis, are visual icons that represent a word or idea; e.g., smiles, winks, happy faces, thumbs up.

Something Borrowed, Something New

"We don't just borrow words; on occasion, English has pursued other languages down alleyways to beat them unconscious and rifle their pockets for new vocabulary."
— Booker T. Washington

Here is a transcription of a recent bit of dialogue at a restaurant:

Waiter: May I take your order?

Larry: I'll have the sushi appetizer. I'd like ravioli with a side order of zucchini. For dessert, a gelato and a cappuccino. My friend will have nachos with salsa, steak frites, and a strudel for dessert.

English words by country or
language of origin
Latin   29%
French   29%
Germanic   26%
Greek   6%
Others   10%

For further inquiry, have students
check out the following website:
45 Common English Words that
Come from Other Languages:
http://www.fluentu.com/blog/
english/english-words-from-other-
languages

This little exchange has me speaking Japanese, Italian, Spanish, French, and German. There is a banquet of words that we have borrowed from different cultures and made part of our culture and usage—particularly when referring to food items.

Many words that have common English language usage have origins from other cultures or language groups (like the Romance languages, based on Latin).

graffiti: *graffiato* (Italian)
Lego: *leg godt* (Danish) (meaning "play well")
lemon: *limon* (French); *limone* (Italian); *laymun* (Arabic)
mosquito: *mosca* (Spanish)
disaster: *disastro* (Italian); *desastre* (French)
denim: *de Nimes* (French)

Some English words are borrowed from other languages and become new and by exploding into everyday usage. Some words may disappear over time, perhaps needing the support of the culture that they come from. By drawing attention to the culture origin of words, we can help students learn about the place of words in past, present, and future social and political worlds.

When a concept is important to a culture, words develop to encompass every aspect of that idea:

- The Inuit have at least 50 words for the word snow.
- Hawaiians have more than 60 words for describing fishing nets.
- It has been said that there are more than 1000 Arab words for camel—but that surely is an exaggeration. It is true that *nakhur* is the Persian word for "a camel that gives no milk until her nostrils are tickled," so maybe 1000 isn't that farfetched…

Exploring Word Origins

A Taste of Borrowed Food Words

Use the Borrowed Food Words template on page 125. Students organize food items by listing them in columns that indicate their language of origin. Then, in small groups, they discuss the origins of a list of food words.

Culture Word Quiz

The True/False quiz on page 126 will provide students with some insights into familiar vocabulary that comes from different cultures. Note: #6, #9, #10, and #11 are false.

Words Borrowed from Indigenous Languages

There are a number of words in English that are borrowed from indigenous languages from all over the globe. Members of the Algonquin group of nations were generally the first to meet English explorers and settlers to North America, and many words from this group of languages made their way into English. Words borrowed from North American Indigenous languages may come from more than one nation; for example, *chipmunk* comes from the Ojibwe *ajidamoo* or the Odawa *jidmoonh*, both words referring to the squirrel and the way it comes down from trees headfirst.

- Most words of Indigenous language origin are common names of flora or fauna native to North American; for example, the word *caribou* comes from *qualipu* (Mikmak) meaning "snow-shoveler."
- Some words give honor to Native Americans or First Nations peoples; for example, *sequoia* trees are named after the Cherokee leader Sequoyah.
- Many place names in North America are of Aboriginal origin; for example, *Mississippi* comes from the Ojibwe word *misiziibr*, meaning "great river."

Etymology of Place Names

The city of Toronto was once named York because Lt. Governor John Graves Simcoe preferred using English names over First Nations languages. In 1834, the name was officially changed to Toronto. The most common explanation for how the city of Toronto got its name is that it is derived from the Huron word meaning "meeting place." Research tells us that there may be other origins for the name: the Iroquois *thoron-t-hen* (fallen trees in the water); the Mohawk *tkanaranto* (place for poles or trees).

Have students investigate the origin of the name of the city, state or province, or country that they live in. What landmarks (bodies of water, mountains, street names) have origins in Indigenous or other languages?

Investigating Indigenous Word Origins

Present the following list of words that may be familiar to the students.

hurricane	pecan	skunk
kayak	pemmican	tipi /tepee
moccasin	potlatch	toboggan
moose	powwow	totem
mugwump	quonset	wampum
muskrat	Sasquatch	

Students are each assigned one word to investigate.
- What is the word in its original language?
- Which Indigenous group(s) introduced the word?
- What does the word mean?
- Illustrate the word.

Students can create a collaborative book of words that can serve as a glossary, with each student contributing one item,

---

Living Languages

Unlike Latin, Indigenous languages shouldn't be considered to be dead; there are more than 70 distinct Indigenous languages in North American. There has been a decrease in the transmission of Indigenous languages from one generation to the next, and strong efforts have been made by Indigenous peoples to revitalize and sustain their languages. It is worth noting that Prime Minister Justin Trudeau passed a law to protect and preserve Indigenous languages in Canada.

On October 27, 2018, a news item reported that Angus Andersen, a resident of St. John's, Newfoundland, uses his Twitter account to expose Inuit language and culture to the world. Andersen doesn't have Internet in his home but goes into town to send out an Inuk word of the day (e.g., *tassijuak* is a saltwater pond). Andersen claims, "I'm doing what an Inuk is supposed to do when they come to a certain age. You learn so much, and now you teach… With one word at a time you can learn quite a bit." The Tweets have become so popular that now have increased to two a day, and three on Fridays.

Words Can Hurt

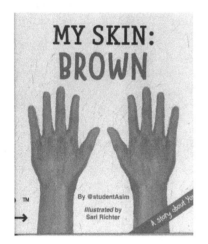

"Ayden, you look upset," said Mom. "Did something happen?"
"Some people called me a word I never heard before," said Ayden.
Mom was immediately concerned. "What did they call you?" she asked. "Come sit down."
Ayden whispered in Mom's ear.
Mom gasped.
…"Mom what does that word mean?"
— from *My Skin: Brown* by @studentAsim; illus. Sari Richter

Author Asim Hussain has created a special picture book to help young people consider the power of words, the hurt of name-calling, and the story of racism that pervades many societies. Ayden is called a word and, when his mother explains that is a "bad" word, he questions who might say this word and why. The word is not made explicit in the story, nor need it be. Many young children have heard or said words that are derogatory or used as put-downs. Such words are considered bad because they represent prejudice against one's race, class, physical ability, mental ability, or gender identity. Children might come to school having heard these words, perhaps having said these words.

When considering word usage, it is no secret that some words are considered bad. It is no secret that students may hear—or use—derogatory/bad/curse words inside and outside the class, both out loud and on social media. It is important that our classrooms be places that provide students with understanding that such words can be hurtful and abusive, and can inflict emotional pain. Being on the receiving end of name-calling can promote feelings of exclusion and rejection. When being called names repeatedly, it is hard to "get over it" without getting help from others. Those who intentionally call others names to hurt can be considered bullies, racist, or homophobic. To shape caring citizens of the world, we need to help students understand that this is wrong.

We can approach this lesson by reading a picture book, sharing a poem, drawing on events from a novel, introducing a real-life incident reported in a newspaper, or watching a YouTube video that helps students consider their moral-ethical stance when it comes to name-calling. Better still, the lesson about appropriateness and hurtfulness can emerge from context, and may best be dealt with one-on-one or in small groups. A colleague always chose to confront a student when he heard him or her using the word *faggot*. "Do you know what the word means?" he'd ask. He'd explain that a faggot is a term for "a bundle of sticks or twigs bound together by fuel." Confronting students, informing students, and challenging students can be, and should be, an important part of our word-teaching.

Our classrooms and school communities need to be places where students feel safe. When hateful, bad words are used in the classroom, in the hallway, or on the playground, we need to confront the students and explain that some words are hurtful and hateful. We strive to build caring communities and students who are compassionate and tolerant of others, so discussion is needed to help students come to an understanding of which words are good, which words are bad. Discussions might arise from events that have taken place in the school community or the media. Often significant discussions about language use and culture can emerge by responding to such stories such as *My Skin: Brown*.

Bookshelf: Picture Books that Help Build Understanding of Differences

Christine Baldacchino; illus. Isabelle Malenfant. *Morris Micklewhite and the Tangerine Dress*
Paige Britt, Sean Qualls & Selina Alko. *Why Am I Me?*
Michael Leannah; illus. Jennifer E. Morris. *Most People*
Julius Lester. *Let's Talk about Race*
Yuyi Morales. *Dreamers*
Todd Parr. *It's Okay to be Different* (also *Be Who You Are*)
Tania Duprey Stehlik; illus. Vanja Vuleta Jovanovic. *Violet*
Elizabeth Verdick; illus. Marieka Heinlen. *Words Are Not for Hurting*
Kari-Lynn Winters; illus François Thisdale. *French Toast*
Jacqueline Woodson; illus. Rafael López. *The Day You Begin*

Inquiry into Culture-Related Vocabulary

Whether we are discussing African Americans, LGBTQ people, or Aboriginal peoples, there are a number of vocabulary words connected to each that need to be investigated and understood for political correctness.

> Vocabulary related to Black culture: *Afro American, colored, Negro, Black Americans*
> Vocabulary related to LGBT culture: *gay, bisexual, transgender, transsexual, questioning, asexual, pansexual, two-spirit*
> Vocabulary related to Indigenous Peoples: *Aboriginal, First Nations, Indian, Native American, American Indian, Status Indian, Eskimo, Inuit, Métis, Amerindian*

Older students may work alone or with a partner to investigate words associated with one of these topics, perhaps highlighting the history of one or more of these words. Students can report their findings.

> ### Political Correctness
>
> When using words to describe particular cultures, we need to be aware and sensitive about what terms are considered politically correct. The terminology we use in current times is drawn from a history of usage over centuries. The rules are often complex, and answers about correctness can vary depending on who is doing the talking, who you are talking to, and what the intended meaning is behind the words we choose to use. Providing students with information and inquiry into politically correct terms can help them be conscious and considerate of using words "correctly." Discussion about proper naming has been ongoing and changing, particularly in the 21st century, and we can invite students to be part of that discussion.

YouTube videos are available for students to watch help them consider the power of words. Students viewing these videos independently can then decide which of them might be useful/informative to share with the class:
• Words Can Hurt You (iSong by Nightcore)
• Words Do Hurt (Alye)
• Words Can Hurt (Bullying commercial)
• Words Really Do Hurt

Providing background information and knowledge about the terminology can help students be aware and care about politically correct terminology.

What is the most politically correct term for Black citizens of the United States?

- The most politically correct term to use is *African American*. The word can be spelled with or without a hyphen. Suggestion: When the term is used as a noun, the hyphen can be omitted; as an adjective (African-American literature) the hyphen can be included. Using the word *Black* is acceptable, as long as it's not said in a contemptuous manner. The word Negro is an archaic term that can be construed as offensive because of its association with the long history of slavery, segregation, and discrimination, and should be considered off-limits.

Is a Black Canadian known as an African Canadian?

- *Black Canadian* is a designation of Black people who are citizens or permanent residents of Canada. The majority of Black Canadians are of Caribbean descent and thus may reject the term *African Canadian*.

What does the term LGBT mean?

An initialism is an abbreviation consisting of initial letters pronounced separately; e.g., ASAP (As Soon As Possible); RIP (Rest In Peace); FBI (Federal Bureau of Investigation).

- LGBT is an adjective, an initialism that stands for Lesbian, Gay, Bisexual, and Transgender. The initialism is intended to emphasize the diversity of sexuality and genderidentity cultures. The letter Q is often added to the initialism to represent Queer or Questioning (LGBTQ).

Which pronouns are correct? he/him? she/her? they/their?

- It's often important to use language that implicitly or explicitly includes both men and women, making no distinction between the genders. This can be tricky when it comes to pronouns. There are currently no personal pronouns in English that refer to someone (as opposed to something) without identifying whether that person is male or female. Gender-neutral, gender-appropriate pronouns have a history of challenging our use of English, but in recent years they have been important to nonbinary people who don't identify as either male or female. Using either "he" or "she" is inadequate, as is the term "he or she," as it assumes binary gender. Some consider the use of "they" grammatically incorrect because it refers to more than one. Still, the use of "they" is becoming more widely accepted in both speech and writing. In everyday life, nonbinary people usually state a preference for the appropriate pronoun; e.g. "My name is Brendan, I use they/them pronouns."

What does the word *indigenous* mean?

- *Indigenous* specifies something or someone that is native rather than coming or being brought from elsewhere. Globally, there is no accepted definition of indigenous peoples. Some countries refer to indigenous peoples as the people who were there at first contact. Others refer to indigenous peoples as the nomadic people in their country. In Canada, the terms *Aboriginal* or *Indigenous* are used to describe all indigenous peoples within the country, including First Nations, Métis, and Inuit peoples.

What is the initialism FNMI?

- According to the Canadian Constitution Act (1982), Aboriginal Peoples includes First Nations, Métis, and Inuit people and is now considered the legal term for describing Canadian Aboriginal peoples. *First people* and *First Nations* are interchangeable terms. Some First Nations prefer not to be called Aboriginal peoples. *Aboriginal peoples* is considered the correct term as opposed to *Aboriginal* as a noun or *Aboriginals*. *First Nations* is a term used to identify Indigenous peoples of Canada who are neither Métis nor Inuit. The term replaced *Indian* for individuals and *Indian band* or *tribe* for groups.

gr8 Texting Words

Examples: RU = Are you?
              SLAP = Sounds Like a Plan

1. 2moro
2. B4YKI
3. BRT
4. C-P
5. CTN
6. CUS
7. E123
8. F2F
9. FC
10. FOAF
11. HAK
12. JK
13. JTLYK
14. K, KK
15. NC
16. NP
17. NVM
18. OATUS
19. OMW
20. OTP
21. RN
22. SITD
23. WB
24. WYCM
25. WYWH

Bonus: What are three text message abbreviations you might add to this list?

Borrowed Food Words

A. Organize these food items by listing them in one of three columns that indicate their language of origin.

	Italian	**French**	**Spanish**
	Example: *linguini*	Example: *frites*	Example: *tortilla*
linguini frites tortilla croissant poutine burrito latte linguini salsa enchilada tortilla crème brulée macaron macaroni pizza pasta spaghetti zucchini frites champagne guacamole tortilla			

B. In groups, discuss what language or culture is associated with each of these food terms.

- schnitzel
- bagel
- dim sum
- borscht
- gumbo
- tofu
- dal
- pierogi
- hummus
- pho
- kebab
- smorgasbord

Pembroke Publishers ©2019 *Word by Word* by Larry Swartz ISBN 978-1-55138-338-5

Culture Word Quiz

Part A

Circle T (True) or F (False) for each of the following statements.

1. DELICATESSEN comes from the German word Delikatessen.   T   F

2. When you say GESUNDHEIT you are speaking German.   T   F

3. KINDERGARTEN literally means "children's garden."   T   F

4. A RUCKSACK, a BACKPACK, and a KNAPSACK are all the same thing.   T   F

5. KLUTZ is a Jewish word.   T   F

6. A PIÑATA is a type of Spanish food.   T   F

7. KARATE is a Japanese word that means "empty hand."   T   F

8. CHOCOLATE comes from the ancient Mexican word *xocalati*.   T   F

9. PAPARAZZI is married to MAMARAZZI.   T   F

10. KHAKI is a sweet Japanese dessert.   T   F

11. A BLOKE is something you wear in England.   T   F

12. If you are going to the LOO you are using the washroom.   T   F

Part B

In groups, discuss which culture or country each of the following clothing items is associated with:

dungarees
hijab
jumper
kimono
lederhosen
poncho
sari
stetson
trainers
yarmulke

8

Word Play

The longer I am in these woods,
I learn words,
I become cornucopic
with language
which rolls around my mouth
like dark chocolate,
like butterscotch
like peppermint
—from *Finding Baba Yaga: A short novel in verse* by Jane Yolen, p. 53

I am very fond of the work of Broadway composer Stephen Sondheim. I listen to his music often and am knocked out when I listen carefully to his clever, clever words. He is a genius at choosing words that draw on events from the story and illuminate the thoughts and feelings of characters. Having written for musical theatre for more than sixty years (e.g., *West Side Story, Gypsy, Into the Woods, Company*), Sondheim is Broadway's most respected composer and lyricist. Here are three examples that show Sondheim's word prowess:

- rhyming "clock turn" with "nocturne" in *A Little Night Music*
- describing a scene in *Sunday in the Park With George* with "That's the puddle where the poodle did the piddle"
- use of alliteration "rooting through my rutabaga, raiding my arugula and ripping up the rampion" in *Into the Woods*

Not many young people will have Sondheim's music in their listening repertoire, but they are likely to have their favorite playlists sailing through their earphones and flying from their lips. There are many reasons why we connect to song lyrics, but wordplay—when words are the main subject of the work, for the purpose of intended effect or amusement—is primary with some songs.

We often laugh at jokes and riddles because they are "punny." When we get the double meaning of the punchline, our funny bones are tickled.

Q: What did the left eye say to the right eye?
A: Between us something smells.

Q: How do you make a tissue dance?
A: You put a little boogie in it?

Q: What is the difference between roast beef and pea soup?
A: Anyone can roast beef?

Other wordplay techniques, such as idioms, spoonerisms, double entendres, and Tom Swifties ("Pass me the shellfish," said Tom *crabbily*.) are part of the culture of humor and amuse us. When we are learning the English language, wordplay can be problematic, since it is dependent on understanding alternative meanings for words and expressions. As ELL learners develop proficiency, they are better prepared to grasp the meaning of a joke or riddle, an idiom or expression, and perhaps to join and smile as they listen or read words at play.

Connected to wordplay is the notion of playing with words. Games and puzzles provide contexts for drawing on and expanding our word knowledge. There is a feeling of satisfaction when we are able to solve the clues in a crossword puzzle, to discover a word in a word search puzzle, to use our Scrabble tiles to gain the most points, and to compete when gathering with friends and family to play board games. When we engage our students with activities and contexts that draw on their vocabulary knowledge and introduce them to new words, we are expanding their wordplay power and their power of playing with words. In this chapter students will have opportunities to

- Learn about literary techniques for playing with words
- Discover how some words are formed to make new words (e.g., portmanteau words, clipped words)
- Discuss and respond to 21st-century words that appear in social media and text talk
- Tell and read jokes and riddles to understand how humor is developed through wordplay
- Play oral and written word games (including commercial board games and online games) to apply word knowledge and to participate in fun-oriented activities with others
- Expand word knowledge by exploring lingo and slang as part of popular culture

> The popular word game Mad Libs is an entertaining way to have fun with words and to practice grammar rules. A reader selects one of the stories from a Mad Libs booklet. The reader asks players to give words that will be used to fill in the blanks of the story. The content of the story is not known to the players; when the story is read aloud, the writers discover that they have written an unexpected, silly, exaggerated story with their word choices. The game can be played independently and is also available as an online version.

Logology = Wordplay

The English language has thousands of words. There are words for words. There are words for words that play with words. Logology is the field of reactional linguistics, which encompasses a wide variety of word games and wordplay. Here is a list of terms that can help us play around with words and explore English in a fun way. As the fish said, "We can participate in logology just for the *halibut*."

Anagrams: Created by rearranging the letters of a word or phrase to produce a new word or phrase; e.g., the letters in *dormitory* can be rearranged into *dirty room*.

Eponyms: A person, place, or thing for whom or which something is named: e.g., *Achilles/Achille's heel*; *Hans Asperger/Asperger's syndrome*; *Walt Disney/Disney-land*

Isograms: Words that do not have any repeating letters: e.g., *trampoline, artichokes, problematic, documentary, lumberjacks, Switzerland*

Lipograms: Writing made up of words that purposefully exclude a letter of the alphabet

Malapropisms: The incorrect use of a word in place of a word with a similar sound: e.g., *coulda* instead of *could have*; *the Sixteenth Chapel* instead of *the Sistine Chapel*

Palindromes: words or phrases that read the same way backward as forward: e.g., *bob, civic, rotator*; *Elvis Lives!, Stella won no wallets, Live not on evil, Pull up if I pull up*

Portmanteau words (also known as blends): a merging of the sounds and meanings of two or more words: e.g., *brunch* (breakfast/lunch), *emoticon* (emotion/icon), *turducken* (turkey, duck, chicken), *chillax* (chill/relax), *bionic* (biological/electronic), *edutainment* (education/entertainment)

Semordnilaps: *semordnilap* is the word *palindromes* spelled backward and refers to words that can be read backward as another word: e.g., *repaid/diaper, stressed/dessert, evil/ live, Oprah/Harpo*

Spoonerisms: a play on words in which consonants, vowels, or morphemes are switched between two words in a sentence or phrase; e.g., *flutter by/butterfly, belly jeans/jelly beans, lack of pies/pack of lies*

In the Classroom: Text Fail Tuesdays
by Shona Scott and Kimberly Ristic, Grade 7 and 8 teachers

I feel that one way to implement spelling and vocabulary instruction in class is to provide a practice that is consistent and playful in the classroom. A task or puzzle is introduced into the classroom each day of the class. This bellringer assignment greets students when they enter the class at the start of the day; i.e., after the bell rings. I strive to keep this a consistent practice, since it helps to address and focus on spelling patterns, words that are demons, vocabulary enrichment, and punctuation rules.

Each day has a different activity, but Tuesdays are the days that we deal with texting; the day has become known as Text Fail Tuesday. Images of text conversations are presented to students as reproducibles or PowerPoint. Students are required to correct the spelling, punctuation, and grammar mistakes in the messages. For example, they correct "u" to "you," capitalize words, etc.

This ritual strategy, I believe, helps make students more aware of the type of grammar and spelling mistakes that are common in text and online conversations. One student told me during our texting lesson that he had once accidentally written *u* on a homework assignment and had had to correct himself. This activity elevates student language and vocabulary skills, using the practice of texting that is very much part of their world as it leads students to become more aware of their own "text fails."

Text Fail bellringers are available from from https://www.teacherspayteachers.com/Product/GRAMMAR-BELL-RINGERS-TASK-CARDS-TEXT-MESSAGES-3517074

Portmanteau Words

Portmanteau words are currently popular in fandom to refer to celebrity romantic couples; e.g., Brad + Angelina = Brangelina, Kim + Kanye = Kimye.

To create a portmanteau word, you take one word, remove a portion of it, and then put it together with part of another word to create a whole new word.

Invite students to write the portmanteau word after giving them two combined words; e.g., hungy + angry = _____

athletic + leisure = _____

chill + relax = _____

brother + hug = _____

education + entertainment = _____

emotion + icon = _____

hungry + angry= _____

friend + enemy = _____

spoon + fork = _____

shark + tornado = _____

staying at home + vacation = _____

smartphone + tablet = _____

sheep + people = _____

Or you could have students write the original words after giving them the portmanteau word; e.g., hangry = _____ + _____

_____ + _____ = brunch

_____ + _____ = athleisure

_____ + _____ = chillax

_____ + _____ = edutainment

_____ + _____ = emoticon

_____ + _____ = hangry

_____ + _____ = frenemy

_____ + _____ = spork

_____ + _____ = sharknado

_____ + _____ = staycation

Portmanteau Dogs

Queen Elizabeth II has two dogs who are crossbreeds known as Dorkies (Dachshund + Corgi).

Many dogs are cross breeds and, as a result, have acquired new portmanteau names. Write the names of these dog breeds: e.g., German Shepherd + Husky = Shepsky; Labrador Retriever + Poodle = Labradoodle.

Pug + Beagle = _____

Chihuahua + Beagle = _____

Maltese + Poodle = _____

Bulldog + Dalmatian = _____

Labrador + Husky = _____

German Shepherd + Pug = _____

Bichon Frise + Yorkshire Terrier = _____

Bernese Mountain Dog + Poodle = _____

Clipped Words

Initialisms are similar to abbreviations and acronyms. They are a clipped way of shortening phrases when writing or speaking. An initialism take a complete phrase or sentence and reduces it to just a few letters; for example, TGIF (Thank Goodness It's Friday; FYI (For Your Information). The term RSVP is an initialism of the French request *Respondez, S'il Vous Plait*, which translates into "Please reply."

Clipped words are words that have been clipped or shortened from a longer word to form a shorter word; for example, a *veterinarian* is most commonly known as a *vet*, *airplane* as *plane*, *telephone* as *phone*, *mathematics* as *math*. Although clipped words are not actually abbreviations, they are another kind of language shortcut. They are one way in which we create new words and change our language.

What's the Long Word?

Over time, we have used some clipped versions of words for so long, we may not always remember the original words. Have students write the original words for each of these abbreviations:

exam	gym	grad
gas	photo	demo
lab	pic	anon
ad	burger	

What's the Clipped Word?

Have students write the clipped (abbreviated) form of these words:

champion	rhinoceros	fanatic
condominium	dormitory	microphone
refrigerator	microphone	limousine
saxophone	influenza	automobile

Clipped Names

What are the common clipped versions of the following names? (Note that some names might have more than one clipped version.)

Elizabeth	Nicolas	Andrew
Michael	Peter	Solomon
Daniel	Vincent	Katherine
Susan	Samantha	

Punny Words

Q: Why was the mushroom invited to the party?
A: Because he was a fungi.

Jokes and riddles are best used when they are told or read out loud. When we read a joke or riddle in a book or magazine and it tickles our funny bone, we are often tempted to share it with others. Many jokes and riddles are written as question-and-answer dialogues. Knock-knock jokes always need one or more audience members to take part. Jokes and riddles can provide an engaging lesson in communication and an understanding of how words work.

When we read or listen to a joke and its punchline, we either get it or we don't. If we are unfamiliar with the words, or are confused by the context, we might not comprehend the joke. In the example above, if we don't know that a *fungi* is a mushroom, or that the word is pronounces as a homophone for "fun guy," then we may be confused by the riddle and probably won't find it funny. There is no guarantee that the joke will appeal to one's sense of humor, but understanding how jokes often use puns helps us to at least get it and stretch our word power.

Exploring Puns

Provide students with the following riddles about animals and ask them to read them with a partner, one asking the question, one giving the punch line. To reinforce the riddle's meaning, have students repeat the activity, switching roles. Ask students: *What makes these riddles funny? Or not funny?* Draw students' attention to answers to the riddles that are invented words.

Q: Where do Polar Bears go to vote? A: The North Poll
Q: What do you call a baby bear with no teeth. A: A gummy bear.
Q: Which day of the week do fish hate? A: Fryday.
Q: What do you call a thieving alligator? A: A crookodile
Q: What do call a deer with no eyes. A: No eye deer (No idea)
Q: Why did the cow cross the road? A: To get to the udder side.
Q: Why do you call a cow that eats grass.? A: A lawn moo-er.
Q: What is the easiest way to count a herd of cattle. A: With a cowculator.
Q: Why are fish so smart? A: Because they live in schools.
Q: Why didn't the little boy believe the tiger? A: Because he thought it was a lion.

Collecting Jokes and Riddles

- Have students use the Internet to collect jokes and riddles about a particular animal (dog, elephant, chicken, pig, etc.). Students can share these riddles with a partner.
- Students can create a comic illustration of a favorite joke or riddle using dialogue balloons between the two characters.
- Students can create a class anthology of animal jokes and riddles, with each student contributing at least one joke or riddle to the collection. The jokes and riddles could be compiled on a class website.
- Create a bulletin-board display of jokes and riddles. One suggestion is to have the riddles displayed as if they were written on a graffiti wall.
- The class can make a joke-and-riddle game by writing a number of jokes and riddles on file cards. The question part of the riddle can be put on one card and the answer on another. Students can match questions and answers.
- Build a class collection of joke and riddle books, with students bringing in resources from home, school, or community library, ordering them from the book club, or discovering them on the Internet. Have the class discuss which is the favorite/best joke for students of their age.
- Students write four or five favorite jokes or riddles and then survey others to find out which they think is the funniest of the collection. The data can be graphed.

• Students make a comedy tape, reading aloud a variety of jokes and riddles for others to listen to or watch. To ensure that the punch line comes across clearly, it is important that they rehearse their routine before audio- or video-recording their joke. Students might choose a particular topic for their comedy routine; e.g., animal jokes, geography jokes, knock-knock jokes.

Word Games

Some of this text has appeared in "Learning Spelling through Games" by Larry Swartz in Booth (1991), pp. 101–116.

My mother made a daily ritual of solving the Jumble™ puzzle that appeared in the newspaper. This game challenges readers to unscramble words that are five or six letters in length; readers then solve a riddle by unscrambling designated letters in the words. In recent years, my older brother has become intrigued with solving Jumble™ puzzles in books. I myself look forward to solving the puzzle in the newspaper, but I do it without a pen or pencil to fill in the spaces.

Crosswords, word searches, and other word puzzles are popular with many people, young and old. When an answer doesn't come easily to us, we might turn to someone to ask for help. When working with others to play word games, students will have the opportunity to develop vocabulary, use logic, test spelling skills, and share guesses and ideas. The games presented here provide opportunities for students to explore and attack words as they solve problems.

The impulse to play games is part of every child's nature. Play is how children spend their free time as they develop their personalities and investigate their world. Playing games awakens the eagerness to learn, to think, to imagine, to listen, to create, and to express ideas. Games, when introduced effectively, can stimulate student interest and can be considered a meaningful event to motivate learning.

Games are basically fun-oriented and, when used in an educational context, they entertain as they engage students to practice certain skills. When used to teach spelling, games can help overcome a child's indifference to (or even resentment of) the work involved in studying, reviewing, or memorizing words. Games can possibly transform negative attitudes into lifelong learning.

Some Online Word Games
• The Pretty Puzzle Princess
• Hangman
• Mad Libs
• Scramble
• Word Connect
• Bookworm
• Word Finder

The use of spelling games provides a medium for learning technical aspects of language, such as phonics, spelling, homonyms, and syllable stress, because games initiate a playful mindset and can make learning about language fun. Since games focus on building or recognizing isolated words, they constitute a substantial spelling program. While launching spelling, the games will, in fact, reinforce word attack and decoding without bad side effects. They are an alternative method for drill exercise or systematic spelling programs.

Word games develop vocabulary, increase semantic and syntactic control, and stimulate logic and imagination. When teachers introduce spelling games into their programs, some of the teaching is indirect; that is, it simply promotes verbal facility. Thus, words that children have seen or heard but never used themselves become parts of their active vocabulary as they play the games. Though the emphasis may be more on gaming than communicating, the meaning is never lost.

Spelling games ensure maximum student participation with a minimum amount of teacher preparation. At the same time, games provide immediate feedback for the teacher, as students focus attention on specific structures, grammatical patterns, and vocabulary. Word games can function as reinforcement, review, and enrichment of spelling rules and can, moreover, build an inquiry into thinking about how words work. Games involve equal participation from learners at different stages of development and can be adjusted to suit the ages, language skills, and background knowledge of the students in any class. In addition, the challenge of competition that is inherent in some games provides students with an additional stimulus to solve problems and stretch their verbal abilities as far as they can.

In the book *Word Nerds*, the authors discuss the use of the Internet (www.edHelper.com) to download materials to make games and activities. By clicking on Create Puzzles, the teachers made board games by entering their own vocabulary words and printing out the game board on paper. The games were laminated, labeled, and stored away for repeated use in the classroom. (Overturf, Montgomery & Smith, 2013, p. 78)

Commercial Board Games

A number of commercial board games are available for students to play to practice their spelling skills, to consider new words, and to learn words from others. Once students understand the rules of the game and enter into the competitive realm of board games, they are participating in what can be a joyful, active experience with words—at home and/or in school.

- Balderdash
- Boggle
- Dabble
- Pictionary (Junior version available)
- Quiddler
- Scattergories
- Scrabble (Junior version available)
- Word on the Street
- Wordical
- Mad Libs

For children ages 6–10
- Articulate
- Bananagrams
- Pass the Word
- Supersleuth
- Word Construction
- Online board games

Oral Word Games

Ping Pong Words

This game is played in groups of three or four. Each person in turn calls out a word according to a topic or spelling rule. A group member assigned the role of the caller and timer (perhaps a two-minute time limit to begin) suggests a topic for the word game. For example: words that end in –*tion*; that include the letter *x*; that are six letters in length; that are the names of cities. The game could be played with two people competing, each ping-ponging a word back and forth. An alternative way to play this game is to work in teams of two or three. Students can be challenged to a competition to see which team has the most words for the topic assigned.

Word Race

Groups of five or six sit in a circle. Player 1 names a letter (excluding *x, y, z*). On a signal, the player on the right must name as many words as they can think of in one minute that begin with that letter. As the words are called, the first player counts them and keeps track of the time. Plurals and repetitions are not acceptable. Then it is Player 2's turn to call out another letter and time the player on their right. The game proceeds in this way until all the players have taken a turn, each with a different letter. The one who gets the most words in the time limit is declared the winner.

Choosy Charlie

With students in groups, one person as the caller announces the letter to be excluded from the answers and gives the first word. For example, "Let's choose a gift for Choosy Charlie, who doesn't want to receive anything with the letter *e*. I will give Choosy Charlie a candy. What will you give Choosy Charlie?" Each player, in turn, names a gift for Choosy Charlie. If the player names a gift already mentioned or identifies an item that includes the letter that must be avoided, they are eliminated.

> Player 2: I will give Choosy Charlie a puppy.
> Player 3: I will give Choosy Charlie a cookie.
> Caller: Oops! Cookie ends with the letter e.

The game can be repeated by naming other vowels or consonants that need to be avoided. Another challenge is to play the game by announcing two letters that Choosy Charlie doesn't like. These letters can be two vowels, two consonants, or a vowel and a consonant.

Are We Thinking of the Same Word?

To demonstrate how this word game works, have two volunteers sit in chairs in front of the class or in the centre of a circle. Tell the volunteers to each think of a word, preferably a noun. On a signal from a referee, players says their words out loud simultaneously; for example, "computer" and "bicycle." Direct the two players to think of a word that comes to mind when they hear those words together. Players do not say their words out loud until told to do so. On a signal, players simultaneously say aloud the word that comes to mind. The game continues until the two players offer the same word at the same time. One of the challenges of this game is to arrive at a common word in as few turns as possible. Players do not have to explain the reasons for their choices. Here is an example of how game might go:

> A: Computer   B: Bicycle
> Referee: Think of a word that connects *computer* and *bicycle*.
> A: Wheels   B: Internet
> Referee: Think of a word that connects *wheels* to *Internet*.
> A: Ride   B: Surf
> Referee: Think of a word that connects *ride* and *surf*.
> A: Water   B: Waves
> Referee: Think of a word that connects *water* to *waves*.
> A: Ocean   B: Ocean

Once the class is familiar with the game, students can play in groups of three with one person being the referee.

Antonyms, Synonyms, and Rhymes

Students are arranged small groups, sitting in a circle. Player 1 calls out an adjective. Player 2 gives an antonym of that word; Player 3 gives a synonym for the second player's word; Player 4 gives an antonym of the third player's word, and so on around the circle, alternating antonyms and synonyms. If stuck, a player may provide a rhyming word as an answer.

Player 1: *hot* (adjective)
Player 2: *cold* (antonym)
Player 3: *cool* (synonym)
Player 4: *warm* (antonym)
Player 1: *fresh* (synonym)
Player 2: *stale* (antonym)
Player 3: *pale* (rhyme)
Player 4: *bright* (antonym)

Letter Switch

Note that this game can also be played in a written form.

In pairs or small groups, one player begins by saying any word that comes to mind. The next player makes a new word by changing one letter. The third player then changes one letter of the newly suggested word. The game should proceed quickly without repeating the same word twice. It is recommended that four or five-letter words be used for the most success.

Player 1: *land*
Player 2: *lane*
Player 3: *lame*
Player 4: *lake*

Word Pairs

There are several words in the English language that often appear in pairs; it is interesting to note that they always appear in the same order. These are referred to as nonreversible word pairs. For example, we likely wouldn't say, "Pass the pepper and salt" or "I am going to see if my sweater is in the found and lost." When we speak, habitual usage suggests that we use word pairs in their correct order, even though it's often be hard to explain why they appear in that order.

This game can be played as a concentration-type game. One word is written on a card and its matching pair is written on another card. The game can be played with any number of words; for primary students, 20 cards (ten word pairs) might be a place to start. Here are some suggested word pairs:

An alternative to this activity: Teacher calls out the first word in a word pair. Students write down the word that they think belongs in the pair. Students can score the total number of answers that were correct.

For younger students

salt and pepper	pen and pencil
black and white	shoes and socks
bread and butter	war and peace
fish and chips	bride and groom
lost and found	high and low
sweet and sour	over and under

See page 140 for a template for the written version of Word Pairs.

For older students

back and forth	rhyme or reason
to and fro	rock and roll
bed and breakfast	pros and cons
forgive and forget	give and take
lock and key	touch and go
supply and demand	wait and see
signed and sealed	prim and proper

Written Word Games

Scrambled Words

This game came be played by having students work independently to solve the puzzle or with a partner to promote conversation and collaboration. A long word (e.g., *concentration, Tyrannosuarus, Valentine's Day, neighborhood, inspirational*) is decided upon. Players compete to see how many new words of three letters or more they can spell in a time limit (e.g., three minutes) from the letters of the word. A letter can be used only as many times as it appears in the word. The player (or partners) with the most words wins the game. Students may wish to score the game by giving 1 point for three-letter words, 3 points for four- or five-letter words, and 5 points for each word that is six letters or more.

Word Chain

Partners or small groups create a chain of words. The first player writes down any word; e.g., *start*. The next person must begin the next word with the letter that ends the first word; in this case, *t*. The next player must write a word must that begins with the last letter of the preceding player's word, and so on. The words are written in a continuous chain without repeating the last letter of the word before and with no spaces in between: e.g., *start, train, never, rodeo* would be written *startraineverodeo*. The game could be played by restricting the rules: e.g., five-letter words, place names, etc.

Categories

Two or more people can play this game. First, each player is asked in turn to name a category, such as flowers, colors, celebrities, authors, cars, etc. As these are named, players lists them vertically on a sheet of paper. The group then agrees on a five-letter word, e.g., *watch*, and it is written at the top of each player's page, spaced so that each letter heads a column wide enough to accommodate the words to be filled in.

A time limit is given (five to seven minutes) and, on a signal, players start to fill in the category boxes with words that begin with the letter at the top of the column. Once the game is finished, players score their answers by giving a point for each word that appropriately suits the category. Note: As a challenge, no points are assigned for words all players have chosen.

Vanishing Vowels

This game can be played in pairs. Each player writes a simple sentence removing all the vowels and substituting in dashes. Partners exchange papers and try to reconstruct the original sentence.

Spelling games can be lots of fun.
Sp–ll–ing g–m–s c–n b– l–ts –f f–n.

Extensions

- The game is repeated, eliminating the dashes:

   Spllng gms cn b lts f fn.

- Students can copy a sentence from a book they are reading to play Vanishing Vowels.

Jotto

Play this game for partners with a piece of paper and a pencil. The object of the game is for Player 2 to guess the five-letter secret word that Player 1 has thought of, while Player 1 is trying to guess Player 2's secret word. The first person to guess the other's secret word is the winner.

Each player writes down a five-letter word on the top of the page and hides the word from their partner. All the letters in the word should be different, and there should be no double vowels or double consonants. Players take turns guessing which five-letter word they think the other play has written down. Each player, in turn, gives the opponent a five-letter word that he or she writes down. The opponent tells his or her partner how many letters in this word are in the secret word. The letters are not revealed, just the number of letters. For instance, if the word is *flows* and your partner guesses *grows*, you say that three letters in *grows* are in the secret word. Players take turns calling out five letter words.

Here is what a game of Jotto might look like:

Secret word: *flows*
grows: 3 letters
great: 0 letters (player can cross out g-r-e-a-t from the alphabet and has discovered that three of the letters are *o w s*, since *g* and *r* must be eliminated from grows)
brown: 2 letters
frown: 3 letters

Tip: At the bottom or top of the sheet of paper, write out the alphabet. If a player guesses a word that has no letters in their partner's word, those letters can be crossed out in the alphabet. The game continues with each player trying to guess all five letters and discover the secret word.

Slang and Lingo

Mr. Stink stank. He also stunk. And if it is correct English to say he stinked, then he stinked as well. He was the stinkiest stinker who ever lived.
A stink is the worst type of smell. A stink is worse than a stench. And a stench is worse than a pong. And a pong is worse than a whiff. And a whiff can be enough to make your nose wrinkle.
— from *Mr. Stink* by David Walliams, page 11

lingo
[ling-goh]
noun, plural lin·goes.
1. the language and speech, especially the jargon, slang, or argot, of a particular field, group, or individual: gamblers' lingo.
2. language or speech, especially if strange or foreign.

Slang is defined as a casual type of language that is playful or trendy. It consists both of coined words and phrases and of new or extended meanings attached to established terms. Slang is most often connected to a particular culture/country, and it can become obsolete, depending on trends.

Some words that we encounter in media, reading, or conversation are particular to the country where they are most commonly used. When in England, you would receive a bag of potato chips if you asked for *crisps*; if you asked for *chips* you would be given French fries. If you are in Australia and are given a *barbie*, you wouldn't be given a doll with blond hair, but would be eating barbecue.

We often meet unfamiliar lingo or slang when reading literature or viewing and listening to media from other countries where English is spoken. Encountering these new words may seem jarring or amusing if we are tourists or hosting visitors from another country, but it is good to know (and learn) some of the lingo to help build our understanding and respect of other cultures.

British Lingo

biscuit = cookie
chuffed = to be very pleased about
cooker = stove
dummy = pacifier
fringe = bangs (hair)
hoover = vacuum cleaner
jumper = sweater
miffed = upset or offended
skint = without money, broke
toilet, loo = washroom
tosh = nonsense
underground = subway

Australian Lingo

bounce = bully
chokkie = chocolate
cobber = friend
footy = Australian football
kindie = Kindergarten
lippy = lipstick
roo = kangaroo
togs = swimsuit
uni = university
yabber = talk (a lot)

Exploring Slang and Lingo

- English Language Learners are often challenged by slang terms because the usage of the word might not connect to what they understand the words to most commonly mean. For example, if someone says, "My dad has some fancy new *wheels*," the word wheels refers to the whole car, not just the tires. If the dad's new wheels gave him trouble, that car might be considered a lemon, even if it isn't yellow. Share the statements below with students and have them determine how they would explain the meaning of the italicized slang word.

  1. I can't go to the restaurant because I'm down to my last *buck*.
  2. You might need to *chill*, so you don't get into an argument.
  3. Your new sweater is *sweet*. Where did you get it?
  4. Just because you don't like sushi, it doesn't mean you have to *knock* it.
  5. My friends and I were *hyped* about going to the concert.
  6. My brother was smiling because he *aced* his exam.

- Students list any slang terms they consider to be part of their country's culture. They can add to the list with words found on the Internet. Have students write a sentence for at least five words or phrases to help explain these slang terms.

Word Pairs

Part A

Pick a word from Column 2 that best belongs with each of the words in Column 1 to make a word pair?

Column 1

bread and _____
back and _____
body and _____
flesh and _____
null and _____
lock and _____
name and _____
lost and _____
nice and _____
prim and _____
pros and _____
pure and _____
bed and _____
supply and _____
tossed and _____
touch and _____
trials and _____
rock and _____
pain and _____

Column 2

found
tribulations
pleasure
blood
key
butter
breakfast
address
demand
roll
easy
go
turned
proper
void
forth
soul
cons
simple

Part B

Discuss the meaning of the underlined word pairs:
1. My mother <u>hemmed and hawed</u> before giving me permission to go.
2. Her announcement is not worth getting <u>hot and bothered</u> about.
3. When the contract is <u>signed and sealed</u>, my father will have a new job.
4. My friend sticks with me through <u>thick and thin</u>.
5. My aunt's baking business is her <u>bread and butter</u>.

Part C

Write a sentence to show the meaning of ONE of the following word pairs:
flesh and blood
signed and sealed
forgive and forget

Pembroke Publishers ©2019 *Word by Word* by Larry Swartz ISBN 978-1-55138-338-5

9

What a Wonderful Word!

The six most important words: *I admit I made a mistake.*
The five most important words: *You did a good job.*
The four most important words: *What is your opinion?*
The three most important words: *If you please.*
The two most important words: *Thank you.*
The one least important word: I

word
A single distinct meaningful element of speech or writing, used with others (or sometimes alone) to form a sentence and typically shown with a space on either side when written or printed.

This chapter is designed to emphasize the potential that providing classroom events that encourage students to be word scavengers can contribute to their excitement and finesse in choosing and using words in their communicative and literary lives. This chapter serves as a synthesis of ideas presented throughout this book and is an invitation for students to consider favorite words, unusual words, funny words, unusual words—and then to perhaps sing out, "What a wonderful word!" In this chapter, students will have opportunities to

- Learn about how some words become popular in our culture
- Discover and develop a fascination for unique, unusual, and/or funny words
- Appreciate words that might be considered favorites because of their sound, look, and/or meaning
- Celebrate their own favorite words by making lists, creating a word cloud
- Conduct research by asking others to tell about their favorite words
- Expand word knowledge by responding to quotations about the power of words

Popular Words

Word of the Year

Word of the Year (WOTY) refers to any words or expressions that have been used in the public sphere during a specific year. In the year 2018, such words as *collusion*, *complicit*, *empathy*, *recuse*, and *#MeToo* gained extensive popularity that was ignited by political and social events. According to an article in *The New Yorker* magazine, the 2018 Word of the Year is not a word at all—given extra punch by the frequent Tweets from the President of the United States, it's the alphanumeric character #.

> "Like most major shifts in communicative modes, # democratizes, while freaking out traditionalists, who worry, not wrongly, about the loss of ambiguity and complexity. But, look, something is being said, and it's being read."
> — from "Words of the Year" by Louis Menand, *The New Yorker*, January 8, 2018

The Oxford Dictionary Word of the Year for 2018 was *toxic*.

The Oxford Dictionary Word of the Year for 2017 was *youthquake*, a noun defined as a "significant cultural political, or social change arising from the actions or influence of young people." The term was first coined in 1965 by Diana Vreeland, editor in chief of *Vogue* magazine, recognizing the eruption (earthquake) within the fashion and music industries being influenced by youth.

The Merriam-Webster Word of the Year for 2017 was *feminism*. The large spike of searches for this word may have followed news coverage of the Women's March on Washington, DC, and other related marches across the continent. News reporters questioned whether someone was a feminist or not, inviting many people to check the dictionary definition of the word.

The American Dialect Society yearly designates one or more words or terms Words of the Year:

2017: fake news
2016: dumpster fire
2015: they (singular as a gender-neutral pronoun)
2014: #blacklivesmatter

The word *syzygy* spiked on the Internet on August 21, 2017, the day of a solar eclipse whose path of total darkness passed through North America. The word is derived from the Greek word syzgos meaning "yoked together." Pronounced SIZ-uh-jee, it is defined as "the nearly straight-line configuration of three celestial bodies (sun, moon, and earth during a solar or lunar eclipse) in a gravitational system." The word will likely not be on as many lips again in North America until April 8, 2024.

Inquiry into Popular Words

- Provide students with a list of ten to fifteen words that have been popular within the past decade. Survey the class to determine which word they might consider to be Word of the Decade.
- Students can suggest words they think have recently become popular. Survey the class to determine which word they might consider to be Word of the Year.
- Invite students to use the Internet to find new words that have been added to the online Oxford Dictionary. Students can provide a list of words, along with their definitions, to create a glossary for this century.

Weird and Wonderful Words

We all carry around a huge vocabulary in our heads. We use many of these words frequently; most we recognize in our conversations and reading; and most we draw upon when writing. Like Eliza Doolittle, we might think we have heard every word there is, but practically every day we come across a new and unfamiliar word that we pause to ponder about. We likely won't need the word in our everyday chatting or messaging, but still we might stop to think about a word because it is interesting, unusual, beautiful, or fun.

Author Yee-Lum Mak collected words both strange and lovely from around the world, highlighting them in a small picture book entitled *Other-Wordly*, illustrated by Kelsey Garrity-Riley. The author, intrigued by the names for the odd and wonderful, for the parts of our lives that are "other-wordly," features such words as the Icelandic verb *hoppipolla* (jump into puddles), the German noun *fernweh* (a craving for travel), and the Japanese *fuubutsushi* (feelings, scents, and images that evoke memories, or anticipation of a particular season).

Weird Words

According to Merriam-Webster dictionary, these are words that have proven to be popular when considering unusual words:

> whoop-de-doo
> defenestration
> flibbertigibbet
> kerfuffle
> persnickety
> serendipity
> gobbledygook
> mellifluous
> discombobulated
> sesquipedalian

- Survey students to find out which words they might have previously heard, read, or used.
- Some students might volunteer to use one of the words in a sentence.
- Students choose one of these words and investigate the definition of the word using the online dictionary. What sentence is used to help explain the meaning of the word?
- What are some favorite words that students might add to this list?

Extension

By completing the Weird Words chart on page 150, students will have a chance to consider words that are unusual or unfamiliar. Students work independently to complete the items on the chart, then meet with others to compare opinions of what others might think are weird words.

Students can investigate the meaning of the words that they checked off to discover their meaning.

The definitions for these words can be found on the Oxford Dictionaries website: https://en.oxforddictionaries.com/explore/weird-and-wonderful-words/

Dictionary Game

The board game Balderdash requires players to devise definitions for unique, unusual, or obsolete words. One person is assigned to write the correct definition, while others need to be creative in inventing a definition that sounds authentic in order to fool the others.

For this game each player will need a dictionary, paper, and a pencil. The referee finds a strange-looking word in the dictionary and writes down the meaning of the word. Then they read out the word and other players are challenged to create a "real-sounding" definition. Each player gives their written definition to the referee, who reads all the definitions aloud. The other players vote for the meaning they think is correct. Any player who guesses correctly gets a point. Each player, in turn, takes a turn being referee and choosing a word; the player with the most points wins.

Funny Words

Include any of these words in a picture book, and you are guaranteed to get a howl from young readers: *underwear, fart, poop.* Any variations of these words (*underpants, toot, tinkle, wee*) is certain to inspire a giggle or two. These picture book titles prove my point:

Vegetables in Underwear by Jared Chapman
Walter the Farting Dog by William Kotzwinkle and Glenn Murray; illus. Audrey Colman (series)
The Underwear Book by Todd Parr
Captain Underpants by Dav Pilkey (series)
Everyone Poops by Taro Gomi
Toot by Leslie Patricelli

Teaching Tip

In classrooms, caution must be taken to not condone the use of inappropriate or "dirty" words. Often we find words funny because they refer to body parts or are put-downs, and the surprise of seeing them in print or hearing them said out loud can be jarring—and amusing. There are many words that people find funny, not just because they sound rude (*titmouse, jackass*) but because they look funny on the page (*gobbledygook, brouhaha*) or sound funny when said out loud (*Bridezilla, platypus, furphy*).

Larry's Five Favorite *Ha! Ha!* Words

1. The first (and probably only) time I heard the word *flibbertigibbet* was watching the musical *The Sound of Music* when the nuns sang about finding a way to solve a problem like Maria, calling her "a flibbertigibbet, a will-o' the wisp, a clown."

2. *Kibitzer*, from the Yiddish language, is a favorite word to describe someone who kibitzes, naturally.

3. I've come to admire/use the word *twaddle* to describe silly idle talk or something that doesn't make clear sense; *piffle* works as a synonym.

4. Describing Uncle Max as a *fuddy-duddy* (a negative word describing an old-fashioned person who doesn't accept modern trends) lets me use an amusing rhyme pair, and is also a true-to-life put down (Uncle Max thinks twerking is a bad thing).

5. The word *nincompoop*, a silly or foolish person, looks funny and sounds funny—and contains the word *poop*!

What's So Funny?

Extension: Have students choose any five of these words and investigate definitions for them.

Display the following words and survey students to find out which they think is the funniest:

snunkoople	schnoz
dingus	nincompoop
titmouse	flibbertigibbet
picklepuss	goofball
bellybutton	snozzwanger

Favorite Words

Q: What's your favorite word, Larry?
A: *Done.*

For me the word denotes
- an accomplishment
- relief at having completed something
- a project (or task) fulfilled
- an indication that it's time to move on (to another task, another project, or rest)

Over the past year, I have been collecting words. I acquired an app that gives me a word of the day (along with a definition), and I've paid attention to words I've heard on TV, heard in movies or plays, read in books, or overheard in conversations. Here an excerpt from the personal word calendar I keep at my desk, in which I record items I encounter through the Word of the Day app, my personal reading, conversations, and media.

New Words Day by Day

Word	Source or Context
ipseity	online research for synonym for *identity*
libtard	*New York Times* article, Frank Bruni
heterochroma	novel, *Edinburgh* by Andrew Chee
equivocate	CNN news
hagiography	review of play *The Lehman Brothers*
sarsaparilla	novel, *Insignificant Events in the Life of a Cactus*
mixolydian	television documentary on the life of Leonard Bernstein
malasadas	*Toronto Star*, food article
perspicacious	book review of graphic novel, *Sabrina*
noseblind	TV commercial
aubade	title of poem by Philip Larkin
terpsichorean	word of the day app; August 12, 2018
egregious	overheard conversation

This word cloud (that's me!) displays my favorites of the words I gathered over a one-month period; with thanks to Randy Kirsh.

Creating a Word Cloud

There are several free computer links that generate word clouds from text that you provide. The clouds give greater prominence to words that appear more frequently in the source text. Students can tweak word clouds with different fonts, layouts, and color schemes.

Students can create a word cloud of interesting words they've collected. Some students may wish to feature words on a specific topic or a specific word pattern. Once completed, students can print out a copy of their word cloud and share it with others by discussing

- the choice of words
- the meaning of some of these words
- favorite words
- how they might alter the design of the word cloud they created

In the Classroom: Word Clouds and Media Identity
by Rachael Stein, teacher-librarian

What is your media identity? Media are such an integral part of our students' life and play a large role in shaping their identity and influencing who they are. They are surrounded by, consume, and produce media for a variety of purposes in every avenue of their life. Students were asked to brainstorm: *What are your favorite media texts? Which media personalities/characters can you identify with? Which media represent you?* They were then to transform their list into a word cloud to represent their Media Identity. By having students contemplate and record words that would best represent their identity, vocabulary and spelling exploration was implemented through a personal—and fun—activity.

In order to invite students into the "media mood," they were presented with a series of images and examples and were asked which one best represented them. For example, there were four sound clips ("When Will My Life Begin," "Lean on Me," "Roar," and "Happy") and they needed to identify which one best represented their life or personality. They were also presented with a series of video games, movies, and film characters from which to choose. From there, students began to brainstorm to create their list of at least 10 media examples. They could use whatever program they wished to generate their word cloud, or could create it by hand. The web app www.worditout.com was the easiest to use, but some students branched out to create word clouds in which the words formed the shape of a favorite media form (e.g. a smart phone), and some imposed their word cloud on a background interface of a media form that represents them (e.g., a computer screen). Repeating a word multiple times in the list made that word appear in a larger font size to emphasize the importance of it in their life.

This assignment was a creative way for me to get know my media students at the beginning of the school year and to get an understanding of their media preferences and interests to better inform my programming. Students were able to examine their own media tastes and habits, to identify other forms that might be of interest to them, and to explore further by checking out the work of their peers. Students were challenged to think creatively and identify media examples and characters that represented their personalities or their lives. For example, they might choose the TV show *Friends* because they belong to a close group of friends or *Grey's Anatomy* because they desire to have a job in the medical field. Students had to be specific with their word selections and thoughtful in their selection of which words should be emphasized through text size and font. This particular media form gave ESL students and special education students the opportunity to be successful in choosing and using and celebrating words in a meaningful way.

Babble, an online magazine and blog network, asked, "What's your favorite word?" Anyone was invited to submit a short video telling about their favorite word in a foreign language. *Papagei*/parrot in German, *Tigerkaka*/Tiger Cake in Swedish, and *Napanoyatha*/bellybutton fluff in Finnish were on the short list of entries. In English the top words were *happy, heart, together, hope,* and—the grand prize winner—*PEACE*!

What's Your Favorite Word?

What are your favorite things? The song "My Favorite Things," from the musical *The Sound of Music*, helps us to consider things that are special in our lives; e.g., raindrops on roses, kitten whiskers, woolen mittens. Similarly, a question such as "What is your favorite word?" challenges us to wonder about words that are important to us. Maybe you like the sound of the word; maybe you are intrigued with the spelling of the word; maybe you connect the word to a story in your life; maybe the word was said to you by someone special; maybe you read it in a book or newspaper or online; maybe the word puzzles you or delights you, fills your mind, or warms your heart. Significant, ludicrous, playful, quirky, elegant—what's your favorite word?

To research this book, I asked colleagues and friends:

> What is your favorite word? What word do you find interesting?
> Explain why in twenty words or less.

Some people responded spontaneously, while others wanted some time to think about it. Ultimately, the research question inspired participants to think about the words in their lives—and to pay attention to words that they encounter day to day.

Students can conduct their own research by asking ten to fifteen people—friends, family, neighbors, etc.—what their favorite word is. Students can share their findings in a chart similar to this one.

Extension: To add to the word-collecting and word-inspecting events in the classroom, each student can share with the class their own favorite of the favorite words.

Favorite Words		
Zachary H.	smorgasbord	It's funny. And delicious.
Jim G.	passion	Suggests a feeling of intense feeling for someone or something. Where do these feelings of passion originate from?
Eleanor G.	OY!	Says a lot (disappointment, anger, surprise) with only two letters, one syllable!
Tom J.	avuncular	Means "relation to an uncle." Uncles are good things.
Steve L.	No worries!	Yes, it's two words, but it says a LOT and means that everything will get solved. This is a good thing.
Mary M.	weird	It breaks the "*i* before *e*" rule. Being weird can be a good thing.
Wendy M.	respect	So important
Debbie N.	love	The word leads to "lovely," "loveable," and "loving."
Joan O.	triskaidekaphobia	The word seems to roll off the tongue and it makes me look smart when I tell someone I know what it means (fear and avoidance of the number 13).
Max O.	thank-you	It's important to be polite.
Lynda P.	cookie	A word that makes everyone smile.
Jennifer R.	idiosyncratic	It allows for quirkiness.
Shelley S.P.	spontaneous	I like the idea that people can have an honest, unplanned, gut-reaction to something.

Elisa S.	altruism	Prioritizes others over oneself. The desire to help.
Lynn S.	drivel	The word stings and makes one laugh at the same time.
Bryan W.	chiasmic	This word means divided and I believe there will always be a divide, whether we know, understand, or respect that divide.

The Power of Words

Many popular authors, philosophers, artists, and political and religious leaders have been known to have written or said things that give us food for thought. When these quotations inspire us to consider the power of words, it is mostly because we can connect the message to our own personal experiences and beliefs. By examining these quotations, students can consider which statements frame their outlook on choosing and using words.

Looking at Quotations about Word Power

Provide students with a copy of the list of quotations on page 151. Students can work independently to answer the following:
1. Which quotation(s) do you find the most interesting? Mark it with a check-mark (✓). Why did you choose this one?
2. Which item or items do you find puzzling? Mark it/them with a question mark (?).
3. Choose one quotation that reminds you of an experience from your own life (or someone you know). Mark it with an asterisk (*).
4. Create a small sketch or drawing for one of these quotations.

Extension

Students work in groups of three or four to share their responses and stories that the quotations prompt. Encourage students to discuss the meanings behind some of these quotations. As a group, students can choose one quotation that they think could best be used to introduce a book about words.

Bonus

Students can create their own quotation by completing the following sentence stem:

Words matter because…

Weird Words

Name: _____

Which is your favorite?

PART A

Fill in the blank with one word to help you consider words that are weird and wonderful.

1. What word do you think is fun to say/hear? _____

2. What is the weirdest/most unusual word you know? _____

3. What word do you know that you think others don't know? _____

4. What is the most interesting word you've recently read? _____

PART B

This activity features unusual words; you probably have never heard of them and they likely will not become part of your language repertoire. To help you think about weird words, answer each question by checking off ONE answer. Once you have finished, share and compare answers with one or two classmates.

1. Which is the silliest word?   ☐ argle-bargle   ☐ peely-wally   ☐ hoddy-noddy

2. Which is the weirdest word?   ☐ furuncle ☐ gaberlunzie   ☐ humdudgeon

3. Which word looks the most beautiful?   ☐ ulu   ☐ eyewater   ☐ incunabula

4. Which is the most unique word?   ☐ gaberlunzie   ☐ futhark   ☐ ylem

5. Which is the most fun word?   ☐ erf   ☐ futz   ☐ plew

6. Which word sounds the most beautiful?   ☐ loblolly   ☐ tokoloshe   ☐ kinnikinnick

7. Which is the most familiar word to you?   ☐ rhinoplasty   ☐ selkie   ☐ lollygag

8. Which is the hardest to say?   ☐ deipnosophist   ☐ adscititious   ☐ borborygmus

9. Which word reminds you of another word?   ☐ boffola   ☐ pyknic   ☐ degust

10. Which is your favorite of these words?   ☐ bawbee   ☐ blatherskite   ☐ mimsy

Extension: Use a dictionary or the Internet to find the meaning of at least 3 of these "weird" words.

Pembroke Publishers ©2019 *Word by Word* by Larry Swartz ISBN 978-1-55138-338-5

Quotations about Words

- *Be careful with your words. Once they are said, they can be only forgiven, not forgotten.*
  — Unknown
- *Raise your words, not your voice. It is rain that grows flowers, not thunder.* — Rumi
- *One kind word can change someone's entire day.* — Unknown
- *Kind words can be short and easy to speak, but their echoes are truly endless.*
  — Mother Teresa
- *All my life I've looked at words as though seeing them for the first time.*
  — Ernest Hemingway
- *The best world shakers are the ones who understood the true power of words. They were the ones who could climb the highest.* — Markus Zusak
- *Without words, without writing, and without books, there would be no history, there could be no concept of humanity.* — Herman Hesse
- *Better than a thousand hollow words is one word that brings peace.* — Buddha
- *Think twice before you speak, because your words and influence will plant the seed of either success or failure in the mind of another.* — Napoleon Hill
- *Words are like eggs dropped from great heights; you can no more call them back than ignore the mess they leave when they fell.* — Jodi Picoult
- *Words can sometimes, in moments of grace, attain the quality of deeds.* — Elie Wiesel
- *Words do two major things: They provide food for the mind and create light for understanding and awareness.* — Jim Rohn
- *I love writing. I love the swirl and swing of words as they tangle with human emotions.*
  — James Michener
- *The most valuable of all talents is that of never using two words when one will do.*
  — Thomas Jefferson
- *Eating words has never given me indigestion.* — Winston Churchill
- *May you have warm words on a cold evening, a full moon on a dark night, and a smooth road all the way to your door.* — Traditional Irish blessing
- *Silence is better than unmeaning words.* — Pythagoras
- *One of the hardest things in life is having words in your heart that you can't utter.*
  — James Earl Jones
- *Be careful of the words you say, Keep them short and sweet.*
  You never know, from day to day, Which ones you'll have to eat. — Anonymous
- *Words aren't cheap. They are very precious. They are like water, which gives life and growth and refreshment, but because it has always been abundant, we treat it cheaply.*
  — Katherine Paterson
- *The difference between the right word and the almost right word is the difference between lightning and a lightning bug.* — Mark Twain

Pembroke Publishers ©2019 *Word by Word* by Larry Swartz ISBN 978-1-55138-338-5

10

A Month of Word Puzzles

Ten minutes can be set aside each day for one month for students to focus on spelling concepts and word patterns. Here is a framework of twenty suggestions for daily word puzzles for a month of twenty school days (not a calendar month). Including this event in the program gives attention to playing with words and provides students with a ritual routine for collecting and inspecting words. This event can be introduced on chart paper, a whiteboard, or an interactive whiteboard, and can take place when students enter the class in the morning, or after or before a recess or lunch period.

This routine, if presented consistently, can provide success for students for the following reasons:

- Each puzzle is designed to focus on a pattern or spelling concept.
- In many cases, there is more than one solution for the word puzzle.
- Many students enjoy the challenge of solving problems in a game-like way.
- The activities are rather short. Students are not challenged to study or memorize the words in any puzzle.

Teaching Tips

- Review instructions carefully, using examples as suggested.
- Encourage students to work independently or with a partner to solve the word puzzles.
- It is important to review the spelling concept introduced with each puzzle, perhaps asking for further examples to reinforce the concept.
- The activity can be repeated at different times of the year (perhaps with a week of spelling puzzles or perhaps after an interval of a month) with individual students assigned to create the puzzle for their classmates.
- Puzzles can be modified by having students reduce the number of items that have been presented.

Twenty puzzles are provided for Primary students; see page 153. Twenty puzzles are provided for Junior/Intermediate students; see page 157.

Twenty Primary Word Puzzles

These puzzles are best-suited to students in Grades 1 to 3.

Alphabet

1. Arrange these words in alphabetical order:

wind	rain
snow	sun
ice	blizzard
cloud	hurricane

Or

Arrange these vegetables in alphabetical order to help make an alphabet soup.

peas	turnips	zucchini
cucumbers	onions	beans
carrots	mushrooms	yams
squash	tomatoes	peppers

Capitalization

2. Give a name to each of these pets:

dog, cat, hamster, rabbit, goldfish, parrot

Or

Write the answer to each of these questions.

Who is your friend?
Who is your favorite author?
Who is your favorite singer?
Who is your favorite story character?
What is your favorite book?
What is your favorite TV show?
What is your favorite movie?

Vocabulary

3. What are these baby animals called? Example: A baby dog is called a puppy

A baby cat is called a _____.
A baby cow is called a _____.
A baby pig is called a _____.
A baby kangaroo is called a _____.

4. What are the plural words of these animals? Example: chicken/**chickens**

tiger	whale
horse	zebra
rabbit	snake
lion	mouse

5. Arrange these words in the chart:

strawberry	raspberry	melon	pomegranate
watermelon	pineapple	lemon	coconut
apple	apricot	blackberry	banana
cherry			

2 syllables	3 syllables	4 syllables

6. Add the letter *e* to the end of these words to make new words. Example: car/car**e**

bar	kit	mad
far	bit	tap
fin	hid	fad
pin	rid	cap

7. Add the word *ant* before or after these letters to make a new word.

Example: pl/pl**ant**, ony/**Ant**ony

gi	import
eleph	ique
eater	conson
ler	brilli
inst	onym

8. Change these nouns ending in *y* into the plural form. Example: key/keys; baby/bab**ies**

party	toy
cherry	monkey
candy	donkey
city	turkey
raspberry	journey

9. Fill in each of these sentences with an animal word that rhymes. Example: *What will you do today?* "I will hug," said the **bug**.

What will you do today?
"I will plow," said the _____.
"I will dig," said the _____.
"I will bat," said the _____.

"I will plant," said the _____.

"I will jog," said the _____.

"I will pull," said the _____.

Double Consonants

10. Each of these food words is missing one letter. Can you spell the word correctly? Example: peper/pep**p**er

chery	buble gum
buter	spagheti
cabage	Bonus: peperoni piza
meatbal	cotage cheese
strawbery vanila	

Syllables

11. Bobby likes to play only things that are two syllables. Which of these 6 things does Bobby like to play?

hockey	Monopoly
basketball	guitar
soccer	volleyball
tennis	drums
piano	hopscotch

Compound Words

12. Match each word in Column A with a word in Column B to write a compound word.

snow	fly
butter	light
pine	brush
tooth	ring
ear	box
eye	coat
flash	ball
rain	man
sand	apple

Consonant Combinations

13. Rearrange these store signs to name things found in a clothing store. Example: sracf/scarf

betl	soksc
sdres	gloevs
shose	jakcet
irtsh	eatersw

Word Recognition

14. These words have been squeezed together. Separate the words to read messages from The Three Little Pigs. Example: Buildyourhousewithbricks/Build your house with bricks.

Getsomesticks.

Carrythestickswithcare.

Benicetoyourbrothers.

Bewareofthemeanwolf.

Hehuffedandhepuffedandheblewthehousedown.

Double-o Vowel Combination

15. The letters *oo* are missing from the middle of these words. Can you spell the words correctly? Example: ck/c**oo**k

hk	ndles
fd	bts
ckie	ftball
balln	snze
mse	bkmark

Adjectives Ending in *y*

16. Add the letter *y* to these words to help the weatherman give his weather report. Example: rain/rain**y**

snow	blow
wind	mess
frost	chill
cloud	Bonus: ice
storm	sun

–*ing* Ending

17. Add *ing* to these things Samantha can be seen doing on her vacation. Example: eat/eat**ing**

play	rest
fish	cook
paint	Bonus: run
read	swim
sail	skip

Consonant Combinations

18. How many words can you think of that begin with the *th* sound? Time limit: two minutes

Vowels

19. Replace ONE vowel in each of these words to a different vowel to create a new word. Example: sh**i**p/sh**o**p

son	share
sing	thank
chop	taken
shirt	Bonus: boot
message	deer
wander	chair
taken	creak
store	

Vowel/Consonant Combination

20. The word *on* is missing from the beginning, middle, or end of these words. Write the correct word by including the word *on*. Example: pd/p**on**d

lg	wder
py	tgue
sg	d't
ir	belg
up	wrg
gg	stati

Twenty Junior/Intermediate Word Puzzles

Double-Consonant Combinations

1. Add the letters *rr* OR *ll* to these groups of letters. Organize your answers in two columns: *rr Words/ll Words*. Which column is longer? Example: fuy/ fu**rr**y

fa	tomoow
i	coect
cay	mior
heo	boowed
piow	huy
yeow	roed
soy	swaow
pu	soow
siy	bae
jey	

Bonus: Add three new words to each column

Homophones

2. Fix these incorrect signs by spelling each incorrect homophone correctly. Example: KNOW LOITERING/**NO** LOITERING

TERN RIGHT
TWO THE WOODS
SUNDAE SHOPPING ALOUD
FRESH KNEW AUNTS
BEWARE OF BARE CROSSING
DEW KNOT FEED THE DEAR
KNOW CROSSING HEAR
WON WEIGH RODE
FOUR SAIL: TOO HOARSES
THE KING RAINS
HIRE PEEK AHEAD
WILL CELL EWE A PALE

Bonus: THERE SEA SIGHED RESTAURANT IS CHEEP.

Alphabetical Order

3. Arrange these word trios in alphabetical order. Example: craze crazy crayon/ crayon craze crazy

pepperoni	pizza	peppers
shell	shellfish	selfish
cheddar	cheese	cheery
should	she	shine
wit	white	what
meant	mean	meander
some	someone	somebody
interesting	interference	infer
needless	needles	new
magnificent	Macleod	Maclean

Bonus: Underline the adjective in each word trio

4. Each of the following occupations ends in the letters –*ist* or –*ologist*. Spell each of these occupations correctly. Words can be listed in one of two columns: –*IST*/–*OLOGIST*. Example: Studies biology: Answer: Biologist

> Fixes your teeth
> Studies botany
> Studies physics
> Studies astrology
> Studies archaeology
> Sells medicine
> Eye doctor
> Cancer doctor
> Hypnotizes
> Is a cosmetics expert
> Is a nutrition expert
> Is concerned about ecology
> Receives you at the doctor's office
> Plays the accordion

Bonus: Can you add two occupations to each column?

5. Add the word *on* to the beginning, middle, or end of these words to spell the word correctly. Example: ce/**on**ce

up	sg	ctainer
pd	ward	natial
phics	wder	cologist
tgue	lgevity	
bd	cstant	

Bonus: Brainstorm a list of words that contain the word *an*.

6. Rearrange the letters to create a new word.
   - Each word will contain all the letters.
   - Each word is one syllable.
   - There is more than one answer for each word.

   Example: miles/**smile** or **slime**

parts	tires
notes	snare
taste	sweat
robes	tacos
steak	spine
races	

Bonus: Can you make an anagram using all the letters in your first and last name?

7. The suffixes –*ible* and –*able* often give us some trouble when we try to spell words. There are no set rules to follow. We often have to learn them by memory. Become a spell checker by examining each of these word pairs and write the word that you think is spelled correctly. Example: **enjoyable**/enjoyible

usable/usible
notable/notible
unbelievable/unbelievible
readable/readible
lovable/lovible
edible/edable
eligeable/eligible

horrible/horrable
acceptable/acceptible
movable/movible
irresistable/irresistible
sensible/sensable
miserable/miserible

Bonus: Add –*able* or –*ible* to these words.

suit
comfort
flex

accept
rely

Palindromes

8. Fill in each blank with a vowel. What do you notice about these words? Example: k_y_k/kayak

w_w
_y_
r_d_r
r_f_r
c_v_c

l_v_l
s_l_s
r_t_t_r
r_c_c_r
H_nn_h

Bonus: Insert *aa*, *oo*, or *ee* to create a palindrome word from these letters. There may be more than one answer for each word.

nn
ss
pp
tt

9. How many two-syllable words can you think of that contain the letter *x*?
Bonus: How many two-syllable words can you think of that contain the letter *q*? Which of your two lists is longer?

Abbreviations

10. Write the words that these abbreviations are derived from. Example: Ave. = Avenue

n.
Co.
Ltd.
Inc.
P.O. box
condo

N. E. corner
Dec.
Sr.
Dept.
Tel.
Etc.

Bonus: Write the abbreviations for these five words

versus
September
Thursday

Boulevard
Association

Alphabetization, Capitalization of Proper Nouns

11. Write the alphabet letters in a vertical column. Choose one of the topics below. Can you find a topic word (or two) for each letter of the alphabet?

athletes
authors
city names

boys' names
girls' names
movie titles

Root Words

12. Choose one of these root words. Make a word web, adding as many words as you can think of that contain that root word. Example: cent: century, percent, centennial, centipede, percentage, centurion

    hand
    foot
    rain
    laugh
    man
    part

    Bonus: Brainstorm a list of words using the word *snow*. Can you find more than 25 words?

Root Words, Etymology

13. Write two or three words for each of these Greek roots. Example: therm (heat)/thermal, thermometer

    bio (life)   geo (earth)
    cycl (circle)   man (hand)
    graph (write)   port (carry)
    mech (machine)   ast (star)

Alliteration

14. Create an alliterative headline of five or more words for a newspaper or magazine story. Example: using the letter *l*/Lazy lizards lounge by a large lake in London. Try these: b, m, p, r, ch
    Bonus: Write a long alliterative sentence that includes your first or last name. How many words that begin with the same sounds can you include?

–air, –ear, –are Sound

15. Brainstorm a list of words that rhyme with *chair*. Once your list is completed, determine which vowel combination was used most frequently. Example: –ear: bear, tear, wear, etc.
    Bonus: Repeat the activity by creating a list of words that rhyme with the word *fear*. Determine which vowel combination (–ear or –eer) was used most frequently.

Plurals

16. Oops! Spellcheck has pointed out that these plural words are incorrect. Become a spell checker and write the words correctly. Example: womin/women

toez	feat	dutyies
childrun	deers	busses
punchis	teath	dices
factorees	radices	

    Bonus: Write the plural form for these words ending in *y*.

story	sky
party	journey
inventory	country
memory	

Antonyms

17. Write the opposite of the following words by adding a prefix. Example: understand/**mis**understand

possible	known
active	appear
able	responsible
honest	approve
polite	regular

Bonus: Add the suffix –*less* to these nouns to write an antonym.

care	heart
pain	home
age	stain
hope	

Word Endings

18. Make a T-chart. In column one, brainstorm words that end in —*ch* (*much*, *such*, etc). In column 2, brainstorm words that end in –*tch* (*watch*, *itch*, etc.). How many words can you list in each column in two minutes?

    As an alternative, you can challenge a partner to see who comes up with the most words for one of the word endings.

    Bonus: Repeat the activity using word endings –*ick* and –*ack*.

Silent Letters

19. Copy these ten words down. Underline or circle the silent letters in each word. Example: thum**b**

ghost	business	mnemonic
knock	gnu	muscle
scissors	pneumonia	Connecticut
knee	parliament	Wednesday

Bonus: Create a word web using the root word *know* by listing as many words as you can think of that include the word.

gh **Spelling Pattern**

20. Arrange the following words, each with silent letters *gh*, into rhyming patterns.

eight	through	weigh
sight	sigh	weight
freight	although	fought
bought	night	brought
caught	light	might
high	sleigh	taught
fright		

Bonus: Write a sentence using any two words from the list. Write a sentence using any three words from the list.

Professional Resources

References

Alexander, Kwame (2018) *The Write Thing: Kwame Alexander engages students in writing workshop (and you can too!)*. Huntington Beach, CA: Shell Education.

Allen, Janet (1999) *Words, Words, Words*. Portland, ME: Stenhouse.

— (2007) *Inside Words*. Portland, ME: Stenhouse.

— (2014) *Tools for Teaching Academic Vocabulary*. Portland, ME: Stenhouse.

Bear, Donald R, Marcia Invernizzi, Shane Templeton & Francine Johnston (2019) *Words Their Way: Word study for phonics, vocabulary, and spelling instruction, 7th edition*. New York, NY: Pearson.

Beck, Isabel L. & Margaret G. McKeown (2018) *Word Heroes: Supercharged vocabulary that powers up comprehension*. Austin TX: Abrams Learning Trends.

Beck, Isabel L., Margaret G. McKeown & Linda Kucan (2013) *Bringing Words to Life , 2nd edition: Robust vocabulary instruction*. New York, NY: The Guilford Press.

Booth, David (2013) *I've Got Something to Say!* Markham, ON: Pembroke

— (2016) *Literacy 101*. Markham, ON: Pembroke.

— (ed.) (1991) *Spelling Links*. Markham, ON: Pembroke.

Booth, David & Bob Barton (2004) *Poetry Goes to School*. Markham, ON: Pembroke

Booth, David & Bill Moore (2003) *Poems Please! 2nd edition: Sharing poetry with children*. Markham, ON: Pembroke.

Booth, David & Larry Swartz (2004) *Literacy Techniques , 2nd edition*. Markham, ON: Pembroke.

Brand, Max (2004) *Word Savvy*. Portland, ME: Stenhouse.

Buis, Kellie (2004) *Making Words Stick*. Markham, ON: Pembroke.

Cunningham, Patricia M. & Richard L. Allington (2016) *Classrooms That Work: They can all read and write, 6th edition*. New York, NY: Pearson.

Fitch, Sheree & Larry Swartz (2008) *The Poetry Experience*. Markham, ON: Pembroke.

Gear, Adrienne (2011) *Writing Power*. Markham, ON: Pembroke.

— (2014) *Nonfiction Writing Power*. Markham, ON: Pembroke.

Gentry, J. Richard (2004) *The Science of Spelling: The explicit specifics that make great readers and writers (and spellers!)*. Portsmouth, NH: Heinemann.

— (1996) *My Kid Can't Spell*. Portsmouth, NH: Heinemann.

— (1989) *Spel… is a Four-Letter Word*. Portsmouth, NH: Heinemann.

Lundy, Kathleen Gould & Larry Swartz (2011) *Creating Caring Classrooms*. Markham, ON: Pembroke.

Moore, Bill (1987) *Words That Taste Good*. Markham, ON: Pembroke.

Norris, Mary (2015) *Between You & Me: Confessions of a comma queen*. New York, NY: W.W. Norton & Co.

Overturf, Brenda J, Leslie H. Montgomery & Margot Holmes Smith (2013) *Word Nerds: Teaching all students to learn and love vocabulary*. Portland ME: Stenhouse.

— (2015) *Vocabularians: Integrated word study in the middle grades*. Portland, ME: Stenhouse.

Paterson, Katherine (1981) "Words" in *Gates of Excellence: On reading and writing books for children*. New York, NY: Puffin, pp. 5–18

Peterson, Shelley Stagg (2015) "Anticipation and Shared Enjoyment of Reading Through Read-Alouds" in Layne, Steven, L. *In Defense of Read-Aloud*. Portland, ME: Stenhouse, pp. 93–95

Phenix, Jo (2001) *The Spelling Teacher's Handbook*. Markham, ON: Pembroke.

— (2003) *The Spelling Teacher's Book of Lists: Words to illustrate spelling patterns…and tips for teaching them*. Markham, ON: Pembroke.

Phenix, Jo & Doreen Scott-Dunne (1991) *Spelling Instruction that Makes Sense*. Markham, ON: Pembroke.

Scott-Dunne, Doreen (2013) *When Spelling Matters: Developing writers who can spell and understand language*. Markham, ON: Pembroke.

Smith, Larry & Rachel Fershleiser (2009) *I Can't Keep My Own Secrets: Six-Word Memoirs by Teens Famous & Obscure*. New York, NY: HarperCollins.

Spitz, Ellen Handler (1998) *Inside Picture Books*. New Haven, CT: Yale University Press.

Swartz, Larry (2017) *Take Me To Your Readers*. Markham, ON: Pembroke.

Weakland, Mark (2017) *Super Spellers: Seven steps to transforming your spelling instruction*. Portland, ME: Stenhouse.

Websites

Rhyme Zone to explore spelling patterns that are rhyme-specific: https://rhymezone.com

Word finder brings up a list of rhyming words of varying lengths: https://findwords.info/rhyme

More Words is best used for searching letter sequences found at the end of a / word: https://morewords.com

Learn That Word searches for Greek and Latin roots: https://learnthat.org

Index